Words Their Way™

Word Sorts for Syllables and Affixes Spellers

Second Edition

Francine Johnston
University of North Carolina, Greensboro

Marcia Invernizzi
University of Virginia

Donald R. Bear
University of Nevada, Reno

Shane Templeton
University of Nevada, Reno

Allyn & Bacon
is an imprint of

PEARSON

Boston   New York   San Francisco
Mexico City   Montreal   Toronto   London   Madrid   Munich   Paris
Hong Kong   Singapore   Tokyo   Cape Town   Sydney

Vice President and Executive Publisher: Jeffery W. Johnston
Senior Editor: Linda Ashe Bishop
Senior Development Editor: Hope Madden
Senior Managing Editor: Pamela D. Bennett
Senior Project Manager: Mary M. Irvin
Editorial Assistant: Demetrius Hall
Senior Art Director: Diane C. Lorenzo
Cover Design: Ali Mohrman
Cover Image: Hope Madden
Operations Specialist: Matthew Ottenweller
Director of Marketing: Quinn Perkson
Marketing Manager: Krista Clark
Marketing Coordinator: Brian Mounts

For related titles and support materials, visit our online catalog at www.pearsonhighered.com

Library of Congress Cataloging-in-Publication Data

Johnston, Francine R.
   Words their way : word sorts for syllables and affixes spellers / Francine Johnston . . . [et al.].— 2nd ed.
      p. cm.
   ISBN-13: 978-0-13-514577-7
   ISBN-10:   0-13-514577-5
  1.   English language—Orthography and spelling—Problems, exercises, etc. 2.   English language—Suffixes
and prefixes—Problems, exercises, etc. 3.   English language—Syllabication—Problems, exercises, etc.   I. Title.
   PE1145.2.J63 2008
   428.1'3—dc22   2008002773

Printed in the United States of America

10 9 8 7 6   [BRR]   12 11 10

Allyn & Bacon
is an imprint of

PEARSON

Contents

Sorts for Late Syllables and Affixes

Overview

Word Sorts for Syllables and Affixes Spellers is a companion volume to the core text *Words Their Way: Word Study for Phonics, Vocabulary, and Spelling Instruction (WTW)*. The core text supplies the theory and research that underlie the curriculum laid out in these companions and it is important that teachers have this text available for reference. The collection of sorts in this book is designed for students in the syllables and affixes stage of development who are usually in the upper elementary grades and middle school (grades 3 through 8). Students who are able to spell most one-syllable words correctly have the foundational knowledge needed to spell the base words to which affixes will be added (both suffixes and prefixes). They will also be ready to look for familiar vowel patterns in the two-syllable words they will study. It is important that students not begin the sorts in this collection until they have a firm foundation in vowel patterns. To figure out exactly where individual students should start you need to administer one of the spelling inventories described in Chapter 2 of *Words Their Way*.

Word study as we describe it is analytic. Students examine words they already know how to read, and sometimes even spell, as a way to gain insight into how the spelling system works. This in turn enables them to analyze unfamiliar words they encounter in reading and to master the spelling of similar words. For this reason we do not recommend that you give a pretest and then eliminate all the correctly spelled words from the weekly routines and the final assessment. Known words provide important reference points for the student who is using but confusing the spelling feature of interest. In this way we help students work from the known to the unknown through the scaffolding process. You may, however, want to use pretests at times to determine if students are appropriately placed in the word study sequence. Students are expected to spell between 50% and 75% of the words correctly on the pretest if the words and features are at their instructional level.

SCOPE AND SEQUENCE OF THIS BOOK

This collection includes 56 sorts and is divided into eight units with a total of over 1,300 words. In the first set of sorts, students will be exploring plural spellings (*-s* and *-es*) and how to add other inflected endings (*-ed* and *-ing*) to words using the "double, drop, or nothing" rules. Two-syllable words will first be introduced through compound words, and then students will study the pattern of vowels and consonants at the place where syllables meet. We call these syllable juncture patterns. Next, the long-vowel patterns that students studied in the within word pattern stage will be reviewed in the stressed or accented syllable of two-syllable words. In a similar fashion *r*-influenced and ambiguous vowels (e.g., *oy, ou, au,* and *aw*) will also be reexamined in two-syllable words. After studying stressed syllables, students will look at the unstressed syllables that occur most commonly at the end of two-syllable words (e.g., *-el* or *-le*) and some of the unusual consonant sounds and spellings such as hard and soft *g* and *c, k, qu,* and silent consonants. Some one-syllable words will be revisited here. Affixes and root words are introduced with common prefixes (*re-, un-, dis-, pre-,* etc.) and suffixes (*-y, -ly, -ness, -ful,* etc.) that change the meaning and usage of words in fairly straightforward ways. The study of syllables and affixes anticipates the more complex roots and affixes that are explored extensively in the derivational relations stage. This collection of sorts ends with a look at homophones and homographs and words with three and four syllables.

The sorts in this collection present 24 words each week, a larger number than many basal spelling programs. The words have been selected according to their frequency of occurrence in reading materials for the elementary grades as well as for their spelling features. Students are expected to spell the 24 words in the sort and understand the spelling principles that the sorts reveal. Reducing the number of words to only 10 or 12 does not offer as many opportunities to discover spelling generalizations or to compare patterns and features. If you feel that 24 words are too many you can, in most cases, reduce the number to 21 by simply cutting off the last row of words. However, we believe that if students are appropriately placed and work with the words throughout the week, using the routines we recommend, 24 words are not too many, especially when they are grouped by spelling features. As mentioned above, if students are properly placed in the word study curriculum they should already be able to spell many of the words, so they will not be learning 24 completely new words in each lesson.

RESOURCES

Word sorts are presented as black line masters that can be reproduced for every student to cut apart and use for sorting. (Enlarge these about 10% before making multiple copies to reduce cutting and waste.) Sorting is an essential instructional routine even for students in the upper grades who still enjoy the opportunity to manipulate words as they look for patterns and relationships among them. It is important that students sort their own words several times. You should also use the masters to prepare a set of words for modeling. You may want to make a transparency of the sort and cut it apart for use on an overhead or enlarge the words for use in a pocket chart. You can also simply make your own copy to cut apart and use on a desktop or on the floor.

Each unit begins with *Notes for the Teacher* and suggestions you can use to introduce and practice the sorts. Sorts can be introduced in a number of ways, and the way you choose will depend upon your own teaching style as well as the experience of your students. The sorts in this book are set up for teacher-directed sorts with the categories already established with headers and key words. These sorts work well when you are introducing a new unit or if you feel that your students need more explicit modeling and explanation. However, if you wish to make word sorting into more of a constructive process in which students discover the categories, you can cut off the headers before distributing the word sheets and use student-centered sorts as a way to engage students in more active thinking. See *WTW* and the CD-ROM for additional background information, organizational tips, games, and activities. You can use the Independent Word Study form in the Appendix of this book for homework.

PLACEMENT AND PACING

This book contains 8 units of study that are grouped by early, middle, and late designations in the table of contents. Following are general guidelines for placing students using the inventory results.

Early syllables and affixes spellers will know how to spell both long vowel and other vowels in single-syllable words on the Elementary Spelling Inventory (ESI) but will make two or more errors when spelling inflected endings. They will be ready to explore in depth the generalizations that govern when to drop a final *e* or double the final consonant before *-ed* and *-ing*. If students are still missing two or more words under vowels or complex consonants on the Upper-Level Spelling Inventory (USI) they will benefit from the sorts for late within word spellers offered in *Word Sorts for Within Word Pattern Spellers*.

Middle syllables and affixes spellers will spell inflected endings correctly on either the ESI or the USI, but will make mistakes under syllable juncture and unaccented final syllables. They are ready to examine vowel patterns in two-syllable words, issues of syllable juncture, and accented and unaccented syllables.

Late syllables and affixes spellers will spell most words correctly under syllable juncture and unaccented final syllables (missing no more than two) and are transitioning into the derivational relations stage, spelling many affixes (prefixes and suffixes) correctly. They will benefit from the study of the most common prefixes and suffixes in words that are easier in terms of spelling and meaning than the prefix sorts in the next supplement *Word Sorts for Derivational Relations Spellers*.

Most units contain spell checks that can be used as pretests to gather more in-depth information about features and to place students more accurately. For example, you might give Spell Check 1 (page 15) to students who are in the early syllables and affixes stage to determine if they can spell words with inflected endings. If students spell 90% on a spell check correctly, then you can safely move on to the next feature. If students spell between 50% and 75% of the words correctly on the pretest, then the words and features are at their instructional level.

The pacing for these sorts is designed for average growth. After introducing a sort, spend about a week following routines that encourage students to practice for mastery. If your students seem to be catching on quickly, however, you can speed up the pace by spending fewer days on a sort or you may skip some sorts altogether. On the other hand, you may need to slow down and perhaps even create additional sorts for some students. Additional words are included for most lessons and a blank template can be found in the Appendix.

In general this collection of sorts might be considered the spelling curriculum for about a 2-year period with time for extra sorts when needed or for review periods. Students' progress through these sorts should be carefully monitored with the goal of building a good foundation for the derivational relations stage to come. Although these sorts are arranged in a sequence that builds on earlier understandings, there may be some cases in which you decide to use the sorts out of order. Some of the prefix sorts, for example, can be used earlier than what we present here.

ENGLISH LANGUAGE LEARNERS

Students whose spelling inventory results place them in the syllables and affixes stage of spelling have mastered many of the basic letter sound correspondences and spelling patterns of English. However, words in these sorts chosen to highlight upper-level spelling issues may also be new vocabulary words to English Language Learners (ELLs) so pay special attention to building knowledge of word meanings. You may wish to reduce the vocabulary load in these sorts by omitting 3–6 words.

Certain features of English may pose confusions for ELLs. Verb forms such as *-ed* and *-ing* as well as plurals and comparatives (*-er* and *-est*) may need to be mastered orally along with the spelling. There should be many opportunities to use the words in speech and writing. Compounding words (*lightheaded, backwards*) and adding affixes to base words (*unhappily*) are common in English but may be rare in some languages. The explicit study of these features and words will be important in helping ELLs master English spelling but will also boost both vocabulary and grammar.

Francine Johnston
Marcia Invernizzi
Donald Bear
Shane Templeton

Unit I Inflected Endings (-ing, -ed, -s, -es)

NOTES FOR THE TEACHER

Background and Objectives

Inflected endings are a subcategory of suffixes that indicate tense (*walked, walking, walks*) and number (*cats, foxes*). Because the generalizations that govern the addition of inflected endings to single-syllable words are reliable and straightforward, we refer to them as "rules." To apply the rules across a variety of words, students will need an understanding of consonant and vowel patterns in the base word. (See Chapter 7 in *WTW* for a complete listing of rules.) For this reason the first sort in this unit is a review of vowel patterns that will later determine whether one must drop the final *e* (VCe as in *hope*), double the final consonant (VC as in *hop*), or do nothing except add the ending (VVC as in *rain* or VCC as in *jump*). Sorts 2, 3, 4, and 5 are designed to help students learn to identify base words and to see how the pattern in the base word must be considered before adding *-ing* and *-ed*. The words in Sort 5 should also be sorted by the sound of *-ed* (/d/, /t/, /ed/) to help students see that this morphemic unit, which indicates past tense, is spelled the same despite changes in pronunciation. Sort 5 will help those students who might be spelling *walked* as WALKT as well as students who read *stopped* as *stop-ped*. Sort 6 takes a look at irregular verbs (*sleep, slept; keep, kept*). There are many more of these words and students can be challenged to brainstorm others, find them in word hunts, and create a class list that can be added to over time.

Plurals are introduced in the within word pattern stage but are revisited here in different words. Sort 7 reviews the use of *-es* after certain consonants (*ch, sh, x,* and *s*) and also looks at how *es* adds another syllable to a word (*box-es, fenc-es*). Sort 8 examines words that form the plural in unusual ways such as *foot* and *feet* as well as words that end in *f* and change to *v* before adding *es* (*wife* to *wives*). Sort 9 explores words ending in *y* where sometimes *y* must be changed to *i* before *-s* and *-ed*. Students will:

- Identify base words and the pattern of vowels and consonants in the base word
- Know when to double the final consonant or drop the final *e* before adding *-ed* and *-ing* in both studied words and transfer words
- Know when to add *-s* or *-es* to a base word
- Know how to spell irregular verbs and unusual plurals studied in these sorts
- Know when to change a final *y* to *i* before adding *-ed* and *-es*

Targeted Learners

These sorts are intended for students in the early syllables and affixes stage who can already spell the vowel patterns in the single-syllable base words to which inflected endings are added. If you feel that your students only need a review you can skip the introductory sorts (1 to 3). You might use Spell Check 1 as a pretest to see which of your students are in need of these particular sorts and which features need to be covered. Students who spell most of the words (90%) on the spell check correctly can move on to other features. Students who miss only a few words will get a review of "double, drop, or nothing" when they do Sort 16.

Teaching Tips

There are a number of ways that students can be introduced to inflected endings and some other sorts are suggested in *WTW* and on the CD-ROM. Additional word lists in *WTW* can help you create more sorts if you think your students need extra practice. Because the inflected ending sorts are designed primarily to teach rules rather than particular words, it is important to challenge students to apply the rules to words that are not in the sorts. For this reason transfer words are suggested for some of the sorts. Word hunts will be especially fruitful when students go looking for words that end in *-ing* and *-ed* in their reading materials. Words like *king* and *sing* might turn up in a word hunt and will give you the chance to reinforce the idea of base words.

Racetrack and the Classic Card Game in Chapter 6 of *WTW* are good for a review of vowel patterns. Double Scoop and Freddy the Hopping, Diving, Jumping Frog in Chapter 7 are designed to reinforce inflected endings. Double Scoop can be downloaded from the CD-ROM. Memory or Concentration would work especially well for the unusual plurals and verb forms that involve one-to-one matching.

The Spell Check for this unit can be found on page 15. The spell check assesses students' retention of the particular words they have studied in this unit; and there is an additional spell check for transfer words.

Because verb forms and plurals may be constructed differently in the home language of English Language Learners, these students may have difficulty perceiving the pronunciation of *-ing, -ed,* and *-s.* The fact that *-ed* can be pronounced three different ways adds to this problem. It is important that students hear and then practice saying inflected words in meaningful contexts such as contrastive sentences that contain both the base word and inflected forms: "I like to **read.** I have been **reading** the Harry Potter books." Help students identify the helping verbs that often accompany the *-ing* verbs. English has many irregular verbs and it will be advantageous for ELLs to study these directly. All students might set aside a part of their word study notebook to create an ongoing list of such words.

Standard Weekly Routines

1. *Repeated Work with the Words.*   Each student should get a copy of words to cut apart for sorting. We suggest that you enlarge the black line masters so that no border is left around the words on the sheets the students receive. This will reduce waste paper and cutting time. After you model and discuss the sort, have students repeat the sort several times independently. The word cards can be stored in an envelope or plastic bag to be sorted again on other days and to take home to sort for homework. Chapter 3 in *WTW* contains tips for managing sorting and homework routines.

2. *Writing Sorts and Word Study Notebooks.*   Students should record their word sorts by writing them into columns in their notebooks under the same key words that headed the columns of their word sort. An alternative is to use the independent word study form in the Appendix. At the bottom of the writing sort, have your students **reflect** on and **declare** what they learned in that particular sort.

3. *More Word Study Notebook Assignments.*   Students may be assigned various activities for the word study notebook as suggested in different lessons. Sometimes it is helpful to illustrate the meaning of words or to write sentences using the words. Chapter 3 in *WTW* has detailed descriptions of word study notebooks.

4. *Word Hunts.*   Students should look for words in their daily reading (in materials that they have already read) that mirror the features studied in the weekly word sorts. After they find examples they can add the words to the bottom of the proper columns in their word study notebook. You may want to create posters or displays of all the words students can discover for some categories. Sometimes generalizations can be made about the frequency of certain rules or features.

5. *Blind Sorts and Writing Sorts.*   A blind sort or no-peeking sort should be done only after students have had a chance to practice a sort several times. Headers or key words are laid down and students work together in a **buddy sort.** One student calls out a word without showing it. The other student indicates where the word should go and the partner then shows the word card to check its spelling against the key word. In a **writing sort,** the student writes the word in the proper category using the key word as a model for spelling as the partner calls the word aloud. After the word has been written, the partner immediately shows the word card to the student doing the writing to check for correctness. These sorts require students to think about words by sound and by pattern and to use the key words as models for analogy. Buddy sorts are a great way to practice for spelling tests and can be assigned for homework.

6. *Speed Sorts.*   Using a stopwatch, students time themselves as they sort their words into categories. After obtaining a baseline speed, students repeat the sort several times and try to beat their own time. Repeated, timed speed sorts help students internalize spelling patterns and become automatic in recognizing them.

7. *Games and Other Activities.*   Create games and activities such as those in *WTW* or download them ready-made from the CD-ROM. Some specific games for the syllables and affixes stage are described in Chapter 7 and other games in Chapter 6 can be adapted.

8. *Assessment.*   You can assess students by asking them to spell the words they have worked with over the week. You might call out only 10 or 15 of the 24 words as a spell check. You might also prepare a sentence that contains several words. Read the sentence to your students and have them write it. Give them feedback about their spelling and mechanics. Spelling tests are provided for each unit in this book and can be used as both a pretest and a posttest.

SORT 1   REVIEW OF VOWEL PATTERNS IN ONE-SYLLABLE WORDS

Demonstrate

(See page 17.) Prepare a set of words to use for teacher-directed modeling. Begin by going over the entire sheet of words to read and discuss the meanings of any unfamiliar words. You can do this by putting a transparency of the words on the overhead, by handing out the sheet of words to the students, or by going over the words on the cards one at a time.

Because only the vowel and what follows is of interest here, the onset or first few letters of the word (which can be one, two, or even three consonants) are not included in the pattern designation. Explain to your students that this is a review of vowel patterns they have studied earlier. Introduce the headers VC, VCC, VVC, and VCe by pointing out that the *V* stands for vowels in the middle of a word and the *C* stands for consonants at the end. Model the sorting of the four boldface key words (*chief*, *wrap*, *smell*, and *whine*). Point out the consonant and vowel patterns in each word and, if you wish, underline those letters in the key words. Sort several more words, then begin to involve your students in the sorting process by showing a word and asking them where it should be placed. Continue with your students' help to sort all the words into columns under each header. The words *quit* and *quote* may cause some confusion because the *u* is normally a vowel. In these words, however, it is part of the *qu* blend and represents the /w/ sound. Contrast *quit* with *bit* or *sit* to help students see that the vowel pattern is VC and not VVC. Your final sort will look something like the following:

VVC	VC	VCC	VCe
chief	**wrap**	**smell**	**whine**
fruit	twig	sharp	theme
brief	when	thank	brave
scout	plot	front	scale
groan	clog	climb	phone
stain	quit	trust	quote

Sort, Check, and Reflect

After modeling the sort have students cut apart and shuffle their cards and then sort using the same headers and key words. After the students sort, have them check their sorts by looking for the pattern in each column. If students do not notice a mistake, guide them to it by saying: *One of these doesn't fit. See if you can find it.* Check to be sure *quit* and *quote* end up in the correct columns. Encourage reflections by asking students how the words in each column are alike and how they are different from the other words. Students should note that the words under VC have short-vowel sounds and the words under VCe have long-vowel sounds. This can lead to a second sort of words by vowel sounds: short vowels, long vowels, and vowels that are neither long nor short (e.g., *scout* or *front*).

Extend

Have students store their words and pictures in an envelope or plastic bag so that they can reuse them throughout the week in individual and buddy sorts. Students should repeat the sort several times using the vowel pattern headers. See the list of standard weekly routines for follow-up activities to the basic sorting lesson. The vowel sound sort described above can be assigned for written work in word study notebooks. Word hunts will turn up many more words that can be added to these categories. Racetrack and the Classic Card Game in Chapter 6 of *WTW* are good for a review of vowel patterns.

SORT 2   ADDING *-ING* TO WORDS WITH VC AND VCC PATTERNS

Demonstrate

(See page 18.) Students should find these words easy to read, so there is no reason to go over them in advance. Put up the headers VC and VCC. Pull out the base words and have the students help you sort them into two categories starting with *get* and *ask*. Explain that these are *base words*. Ask if they notice anything about all the base words (e.g., they all have one vowel that is usually short; they are all verbs). Then match the *-ing* form of the word to each base word. Ask the students what happened to the base word *get* before the *-ing* was added. They should notice that the final letter doubled.

Repeat with several more words in the column. Introduce the term *double* and ask them what is the same about the words that double (they end in one vowel and one consonant). Put the header *double* above the word *getting*. Then ask what they notice about the *-ing* words in the other column and ask them why this might be so. Guide them to notice that the *-ing* was just added without any change. Add the header *nothing*. The final sort will look something like the following:

VC	double	VCC	nothing
get	**getting**	**ask**	**asking**
swim	swimming	yell	yelling
run	running	rest	resting
sit	sitting	stand	standing
shut	shutting	pass	passing
		jump	jumping
		pick	picking

Sort, Check, and Reflect

After modeling the sort with the group, have students repeat the sort under your supervision using the same headers and key words. Have them check their sort by looking for the pattern in each column. Encourage the students to reflect by asking them how the words in each column are alike and what they have learned about adding *-ing* to base words. Have the students put the rules into their own words. You may want to write this rule on chart paper and post it for reference. Leave space for the additional rules and revisions that will develop over the weeks to come.

Extend

Students should repeat this sort several times and work with the words using some of the weekly routines listed above. Word hunts will turn up lots of words that can be added to these categories, but students will find many words that do not fit either of them. Tell your students to add these words to a third column (oddballs) and challenge them to see if they can discover the rule that governs these other words in anticipation of the sort for next week.

Students might be encouraged to write contrasting sentences for the base word and its *-ing* form: *I swim on a team. I have been swimming for three years.* Ask students to share sentences using the *-ing* form and ask them if they notice anything (using *-ing* as a verb often requires helping verbs such as *am, have been, was*, etc.).

Give students additional words and ask them to apply the rule. Some suggested transfer words are: *drip, hunt, tug, kick, stir, mop, wink, quit, wish, sob, guess, smell, chop, drag*, and *purr*.

SORT 3   ADDING -*ING* TO WORDS WITH VCe AND VVC PATTERNS

Demonstrate

(See page 19.) Introduce this sort in a manner similar to Sort 2. Ask the students what happened to the base word *use* before the *-ing* was added. Look at the other words under the VCe header to see how the *e* is missing in each inflected word. Introduce the term "*e*-drop" and put it at the top of the column. Explain that when a base word ends in silent *e* we must drop the *e* before adding *-ing*. Guide students to notice that the *-ing* was just added without any change to the VVC words. The sort will look something like the following:

VCe	e-drop	VVC	nothing
use	**using**	**eat**	**eating**
close	closing	moan	moaning
write	writing	dream	dreaming
wave	waving	look	looking
trade	trading	clean	cleaning
skate	skating	mail	mailing

Sort, Check, Reflect, and Extend

Students should repeat the sort using the same headers and key words. Encourage the students to reflect by asking them how the words in each column are alike and what they have learned about adding *-ing* to base words. Review what they learned in the previous sort and add to the chart. Give students additional words and ask them to apply the rule. Some suggested transfer words are: *ride, need, give, bake, peek, smile, vote, bloom, scream, joke,* and *come.*

SORT 4   REVIEW OF DOUBLE, *E*-DROP, AND NOTHING

Demonstrate

(See page 20.) Explain to students that they will review adding *-ing* to base words this week. You might let students do this sort independently. For a teacher-directed sort put up the headers *double, e-drop,* and *nothing.* Place the key words *setting, hiking,* and *reading* under each header. Ask the students to identify the base word in each key word and then to determine what was done to the base word before the *-ing* was added. You may want to underline the base word in each key word. Sort one more word under each key word and then sort the rest of the words with student help. *Fixing* should be under the header *nothing* for right now.

double	e-drop	nothing	oddball
setting	**hiking**	**reading**	
cutting	moving	adding	
stopping	living	spelling	
begging	coming	floating	
grinning	having	feeling	
jogging	taking	talking	
humming		pushing	
		fixing**	
		working	
		going**	
		snowing**	

**These will become oddballs after the second sort.

Guide the students to reflect on how the words in each column are alike. They may notice that the base words under *double* have the VC pattern and those under *e-drop* have the VCe pattern. However, under *nothing* there are a number of different patterns. These can be sorted out in a second sort. Headers are not provided, but you can create them if you feel they are needed. A second sort of the *nothing* column will look something like the following:

VVC	VCC	oddball
reading	spelling	snowing
floating	talking	going
feeling	pushing	fixing
	adding	
	working	

The words *going*, *snowing*, and *fixing* should raise questions. Although *snowing* might appear to be a VC word that requires doubling, the final *w* does not double because it is acting as part of a vowel pattern rather than as a consonant. *Fixing* has the VC pattern but does not double. This is a rare exception to the rule. Have students think of other words that end in *x* such as *box* or *mix*. Show them that these words do not double because double *x* is not a pattern that occurs in English (*x* represents the blend of two letters: *k* + *s*). This sort will take some discussion but ultimately what we want students to see is that in most cases the *-ing* is simply added to the word and it is only when a word fits the VC or VCe pattern that a change to the base word is needed.

Sort, Check, and Reflect

After modeling the sorts have students repeat the first sort using the headers *double, e-drop,* or *nothing*. The only real oddball is *fixing* because it does not double as expected. To reinforce the idea of base words you might ask students to underline them. Help the students articulate a rule that covers all the words. This may be a revision to former rules.

Extend

You might sort all the words from lessons 2, 3, and 4 by "double, *e*-drop, or nothing" as a review. Students should look back at word hunts from the previous weeks to find odd-ball words they can now sort into one of the three categories. (Even words such as *chewing, seeing, flying, studying,* etc., which have patterns different from the ones included in these sorts, can go under *nothing*.) Add to the list of rules that you have been generating after each sort. Double Scoop and Freddy the Hopping, Diving, Jumping Frog in Chapter 7 are designed to reinforce inflected endings. Double Scoop can be downloaded from the CD-ROM.

Give students additional words and ask them to apply the rules. Some suggested transfer words are: *slip, row, sneeze, pout, find, mix, tap, blow, cheer, love, speed, dress, start, box, draw,* and *win*.

SORT 5   ADDING *-ED* TO WORDS

Demonstrate, Sort, Check, and Reflect

(See page 21.) You might begin this sort by asking your students to spell *hopped* and then *hoped*. Ask them to justify why they spelled these words as they did and see if they can generalize from what they learned doing the *-ing* sorts. Explain that students often have trouble with these words and that the sort for this week will help them learn and remember the rules that govern the addition of *-ed* just as they did for *-ing*. Students can sort without the headers for a student-centered sort, or you can begin a teacher-directed sort using the headers. Asking students to underline the base word may be helpful in determining patterns, especially in words like *hoped* and *saved*. Help the students see that the rules are similar to the rules for adding *-ing* and can be summed up as "double, *e*-drop, or nothing."

Talk about the fact that adding *-ed* means that something has already happened and that such words are said to be in the "past tense." Model, and then have students create, sentences that include the base word and the past tense: *Don't step in that hole. I stepped in it yesterday and sprained my ankle.*

double	e-drop	nothing	oddball
hopped	**hoped**	**joined**	mixed
planned	saved	waited	chewed
grabbed	closed	seemed	
nodded	scored	shouted	
stepped	lived	passed	
dropped	named	wanted	
stirred		acted	
		helped	
		started	

Extend

Challenge your students to sort these words in a second sort by the sound of the *-ed* ending as shown below. ELLs may have difficulty doing this so pair them up with native English speakers to assist in pronunciation. This sound sort will help students see that even when a word sounds like it should be spelled with a *t*, as in WALKT for *walked*, the past tense must be spelled with *-ed*. No headers are provided for this sort but are indicated here for clarity. Ask students if they can see any letter patterns in the base words in each column. They might notice that certain consonants precede certain sounds (*p* before /t/, *d* and *t* before /ed/) and that the words in the last column have added a syllable to the base word.

/t/		/d/		/id/
hopped	mixed	planned	lived	nodded
stepped		grabbed	joined	waited
dropped		closed	seemed	shouted
hoped		scored	stirred	acted
passed		named	chewed	wanted
helped		saved		started

Ask students to apply their knowledge by adding *-ed* to additional words: *march, tame, beg, clean, wave, boil, clip, name, mail, scoop, call, talk, climb, snap, melt, shove, show, thaw, race,* and *pet.* Students could also add *-ing* to these words. Challenge them to write sentences that use all three tenses: *Can you help me? I helped you yesterday and I will probably be helping you tomorrow.*

SORT 6   UNUSUAL PAST TENSE WORDS

Demonstrate, Sort, Check, and Reflect

(See page 22.) Most of these words are not hard to spell, but this sort will help students see that not all verbs form the past tense by adding *-ed*. This may be an especially helpful sort for students whose native language is not English. Introduce the sort by putting up the headers and matching the present and past tenses of each verb as shown below. Explain that these words are called "irregular verbs."

present	past		present	past
sleep	**slept**		sweep	swept
keep	kept		drive	drove
slide	slid		bleed	bled
shine	shone		know	knew
freeze	froze		throw	threw
draw	drew		say	said

Extend

Challenge your students to come up with a way to sort the pairs of words into categories that reflect the kind of spelling change that was made to the word. Following is a possible sort.

Long to short	Vowel change	Change to *ew*	*eep* to *ept*	
slide slid	shine shone	know knew	sleep slept	say said
bleed bled	drive drove	throw threw	keep kept	
	freeze froze	draw drew	sweep swept	

Students should describe the categories in their own way and brainstorm additional words that could be added in each one. There are many irregular verbs, and students might set aside a part of their word study notebook to add others over time. For a complete list check the internet. One source is http://www.englishpage.com/irregularverbs/irregularverbs.html.

Additional Words. *feed/fed, meet/met, write/wrote, rise/rose, ride/rode, grow/grew, catch/caught, seek/sought, pay/paid, lay/laid.*

Note: The past tenses of *lay, pay,* and *say* are all formed the same way (*laid, paid, said*), so maybe *said* is not so strange after all!

SORT 7   PLURAL ENDINGS: ADDING -*ES*

Demonstrate, Sort, Check, and Reflect

(See page 23.) Be sure the students can read the words and know the meaning of each. Talk about how the words are alike. (They are all plurals or mean more than one.) Remind students that to make a word plural either -*s* or -*es* is added. Sort the words first by these two headers. Students will need to think about the base word in order to make this distinction. Because all the words end in -*es* we recommend underlining the base word. This will help students see that the *e* is not dropped before *s* as it is before -*ed* and -*ing*. Read the words in columns and point out that adding -*es* adds another syllable. The oddball in this sort is *clothes*. It is not really a plural of *cloth* but it is a plural, and the -*es* does not add another syllable.

Push the words that simply added -*s* to the side and ask students what they notice about the base words in the words that are left. Focus their attention on the last one or two letters. Model the next step of the sort by placing *benches, brushes, foxes,* and *guesses* into separate categories. Create headers for these if you want by underlining the *ch* in *benches*, the *sh* in *brushes*, and so on, or by creating headers like the ones below. After completing the sort as shown below, ask students how the words in each column are alike. Help students articulate a rule (add -es to words that end in *ch*, *sh*, *x*, and *s*) and add it to the class chart. Because adding -es to make a word plural adds the syllable /ez/ to the word, students should have little difficulty spelling the plural form.

add -es				add -s	oddball
-ch	*-sh*	*-x*	*-s*		
benches	brushes	foxes	guesses	**horses**	clothes*
speeches	splashes	mixes	kisses	voices	
scratches	crashes		classes	changes	
churches	ashes			places	
peaches	leashes				
sketches					
ditches					
branches					
watches					

*Among the top 300 high-frequency words

Extend

Give students transfer words to practice applying the rules: *switch, house, glass, glove, choice, witch, song, flame, pass, match, smash, box, mess, shape, lunch, sandwich, grade, wish, eyelash, drink,* and *mask.*

SORT 8   UNUSUAL PLURALS

Demonstrate, Sort, Check, and Reflect

(See page 24.) Explain to your students that just as with irregular verbs, some words form plurals in unusual ways. Begin this sort by matching singular and plural forms. Take it further by introducing the headers and sorting pairs of words into those that end in *f* and form the plural by changing the *f* to *v* and adding -es and those that make a change in the vowel. There are also words like *deer* and *sheep* that can represent either singular or plural.

fe > ves		vowel change		no change
wife	**wives**	**foot**	**feet**	**sheep**
leaf	leaves	woman*	women	deer
loaf	loaves	mouse	mice	
life	lives	tooth	teeth	
wolf	wolves	goose	geese	
knife	knives			

*Among the top 300 high-frequency words

Extend

Students may have a hard time finding more of these unusual plurals in a word hunt, but some others include: *halves, calves, shelves, elves, ourselves, scarves, man/men, child/children,* and *fish*. Some of these might be assigned as transfer words. Students can be asked to write the plural of *half, calf, shelf, elf,* and *scarf* to apply what they have learned.

SORT 9   Y + INFLECTED ENDINGS

Demonstrate, Sort, Check, and Reflect

(See page 25.) "Change the *y* to *i* and add *es*" has a nice ring to it but the rule is a little more complicated than that. The *y* is only changed to *i* when it follows a consonant (*fly* to *flies*) but not when it follows a vowel (*boy* to *boys*). This sort will help students discover when to change the *y* to *i*. We go back to base words as a starting point and the first sort should match up the base word and each of its inflected forms as shown below. Then organize the sets by the words that simply add the inflected endings (-*ay* and -*oy*) and those that change the *y* to *i* (-*y*).

base	+ s	+ ed	+ ing	base	+ es	+ ed	+ ing
play	plays	played	playing	fry	fries	fried	frying
stay	stays	stayed	staying	cry	cries	cried	crying
spray	sprays	sprayed	spraying	spy	spies	spied	spying

Pose questions that will get your students thinking about the spelling changes. Compare *play* and *fry*. They both end in *y* but one ends in an -*ay*. What happened before the -*s*, -*ed*, and -*ing* were added to each? Speculate about why the *y* doesn't change to *i* before -*ing*. (Double *i*s are rare in English and would look odd. *Skiing* is an exception.) Some suggested transfer words are: *fly* (but not *flied-flew*), *dry, try, prey, slay, stray,* and *pray*.

Extend

After many sorts that focus on base words and inflected endings, your chart of rules may look quite complicated. Now is the time to review and simplify it. The following are really the only rules students need to remember, for now, that cover most cases.

>   **Double.** When a word ends in one vowel and one consonant, you **double** the consonant before adding -*ed* and -*ing*.
>   **E-Drop.** When a word ends in silent *e*, you **drop** the *e* before adding -*ing* and -*ed*.
>   **Change *y* to *i*.** When a word ends in a consonant and a *y*, you **change the *y* to *i*** before adding -*ed* or -*es*.
>   **Nothing.** Otherwise, just **do nothing** and add the ending.
>   **Add *es*.** To make words plural that end in *s, sh, ch,* or *x*.

Students can review all of these rules by sorting words from previous sorts into these categories. This is a good time to play games that will reinforce these rules such as Double Scoop and Freddy the Hopping, Diving, Jumping Frog described in *WTW*. Adapt this game to review all of the rules.

SPELL CHECK 1   ASSESSMENT FOR INFLECTED ENDINGS

The words below have been selected from previous lessons. (You may want to use different ones.) Call them aloud for students to spell on a sheet of notebook paper.

1. swimming	2. eating	3. fries	4. living
5. fixing	6. stayed	7. dropped	8. foxes
9. helped	10. spelling	11. leaves	12. plays
13. named	14. stirred	15. crying	16. swept
17. wolves	18. watches	19. grabbed	20. humming

Transfer Test.   Students should be expected not only to spell words from previous sorts but also to apply their understanding of how to add inflected endings to other base words. In this assessment students will be asked to add *-s, -ed,* and *-ing* to given base words. Alert students to the fact that there are a couple of irregular verbs (*said* and *flew*). A prepared assessment form can be found on page 26. The final paper should look like the following:

Base word	Add *-s* or *-es*	Add *-ed*	Add *-ing*
1. trip	trips	tripped	tripping
2. chase	chases	chased	chasing
3. need	needs	needed	needing
4. dress	dresses	dressed	dressing
5. dry	dries	dried	drying
6. tax	taxes	taxed	taxing
7. fan	fans	fanned	fanning
8. race	races	raced	racing
9. say	says	said*	saying
10. fly	flies	flew*	flying

*Irregular verb whose past tense is not formed with *-ed.*

SORT 1   Review of Vowel Patterns in One-Syllable Words

VVC	VC	VCC	VCe
chief	wrap		smell
whine	fruit		twig
sharp	theme		brief
when	thank		brave
scout	plot		front
scale	groan		clog
climb	phone		stain
quit	trust		quote

SORT 2   Adding *-ing* to Words with VC and VCC Patterns

VC	VCC	double	nothing
get	**getting**		**ask**
asking	swim		yell
swimming	rest		run
sit	yelling		resting
stand	running		pass
sitting	pick		standing
jump	shut		picking
shutting	passing		jumping

SORT 3 Adding -ing to Words with VCe and VVC Patterns

VCe	VVC	e-drop	nothing
use	using		eat
eating	close		moan
wave	writing		dreaming
looking	dream		skate
closing	trading		cleaning
clean	write		moaning
trade	skating		waving
look	mail		mailing

SORT 4   Review of Double, *e*-Drop, and Nothing

double	*e*-drop	nothing	*oddball*
setting	**hiking**	**reading**	
floating	cutting	moving	
stopping	living	spelling	
coming	begging	adding	
grinning	having	feeling	
jogging	taking	talking	
pushing	humming	working	
fixing	going	snowing	

SORT 5   Adding *-ed* to Words

double	*e*-drop	nothing	*oddball*
hopped	**hoped**	**joined**	
acted	planned	saved	
waited	wanted	grabbed	
closed	mixed	helped	
nodded	scored	shouted	
started	stirred	stepped	
named	passed	dropped	
chewed	lived	seemed	

SORT 6   Unusual Past Tense Words

present	past	
sleep	slept	keep
slide	shine	freeze
sweep	bleed	throw
know	threw	drew
knew	bled	swept
froze	draw	shone
say	slid	said
drove	kept	drive

SORT 7   Plural Endings: Adding -es

add -*es*	add -*s*	*oddball*
benches	**horses**	foxes
guesses	brushes	speeches
splashes	scratches	clothes
mixes	churches	crashes
voices	peaches	classes
kisses	sketches	ditches
leashes	changes	branches
watches	places	ashes

SORT 8   Unusual Plurals

fe > *ves*	vowel change	no change
wife	**wives**	**sheep**
foot	feet	loaf
lives	women	leaves
leaf	geese	woman
mouse	loaves	life
wolves	mice	goose
knives	knife	wolf
tooth	deer	teeth

SORT 9   y + Inflected Endings

base word	+ *s*	+ *ed*	+ *ing*
play	fry		stays
crying	plays		fried
sprays	fries		played
playing	frying		spies
staying	sprayed		cries
spraying	cry		spied
spy	stay		stayed
cried	spray		spying

Transfer Test for Sorts 1–9

Name _____

Directions: Add the ending to the base word. Don't forget to look at the pattern and spelling of the base word to determine what changes might be needed.

Base word	Add -s or -es	Add -ed	Add -ing
1. trip			
2. chase			
3. need			
4. dress			
5. dry			
6. tax			
7. fan			
8. race			
9. say			
10. fly			

Unit II   Compound Words

NOTES FOR THE TEACHER

Background and Objectives

Compound words show up early in children's reading and teachers should be ready to talk about such words when they arise. Spelling compound words is not especially challenging **if** students know how to spell the two words that make up the compound word. For this reason we have left the formal study of compound words to the early syllables and affixes stage when students have learned the patterns in one-syllable words. By doing it here we want to introduce the idea that there are familiar parts within longer words that will make those words easier to understand, read, and spell—some of the key understandings of this stage. Students will:

- Be able to identify and define compound words as words that are made up of two other words
- Be able to spell the words in these sorts

We offer only two sorts here in this short unit, one made up of some words that are concrete and easy to spell and another that contains a collection of less concrete words. This should be enough to introduce the term "compound words" and to get your students attuned to looking for them in later sorts and in the reading and writing they do all the time. No spell check is included for this short unit.

Targeted Learners

These sorts can be used anytime, but students in the early syllables and affixes stage should already be able to spell the two words that make up the compound word and can explore the meanings of the words. These sorts might be especially helpful to ELLs who will benefit from the attention paid to word meanings. Not all languages create words by compounding so some explicit instruction with this feature of English is important.

Teaching Tips

Use the same weekly routines described on pages 6–7 with some modifications. Rather than hunting for words that fit the specific categories established with the words in the sort (e.g., more words with *light*), word hunts can focus on finding any compound words.

Give students one word (like *man*) and challenge them to come up with as many compound words as possible (*manmade, manhole, manhandle*, etc.). Brainburst, described in Chapter 8 of *WTW*, can make the brainstorming described above into a game using these suggested words: *man, air, back, eye, hand, foot, home, horse, house, land, life, night, out, over, play, road, sand, sea, under, water*, and *wind*.

Students often enjoy illustrating the meaning of both the words that make up the compound words as well as the final word (*snow + man = snowman*). Ask your students to pick five words and draw a picture that will make the meaning clear. Such drawings might be displayed or collected into a class book. You might also create a version of Homophone Win, Lose, or Draw, described in Chapter 6 of *WTW*, that features compound words.

Students can be challenged to set apart a section of their word study notebooks to record more compound words they might find (the list of compound words in the Appendix of *WTW* is only a small sample), or the class might create a bulletin board or chart that is added to during the entire year. Hyphenated words might be added as well, because these are often confused with compound words. (Is it *goodbye* or *good-bye*?) Rick Walton has created a list of more than 2,000 compound words at www.rickwalton. com/curricul/compound.htm, but it will be more meaningful if your students become compound word detectives who are constantly looking for them in their readings.

SORT 10   COMPOUND WORDS

Demonstrate

(See page 30.) This is a good collection of words to use for a student-centered sort. Show your students all the words without going over the meanings in advance (that will come later). Ask them for ideas about how to sort these words into categories. Students should quickly spot the common elements, but if they do not, be ready to model each category. Note that the word *headlight* can be sorted in two different places. Review the term "compound words" with your students and help them develop their own definition based on the words they see in the sort. After sorting, discuss the meaning of the words and how the meaning relates to the two words that make it up: *A bookmark marks your place in a book; Sunlight is the light that comes from the sun*, and so on. Some compound words cannot be interpreted so literally. *Headstrong* does not literally mean "strong in the head" but rather "strong willed." Ask students to look up the meaning of a few words such as this one as part of the group discussion. The sort will look something like the following:

bookcase	**light**house	**down**hill	**head**ache	**snow**man
bookmark	lightweight	downstairs	headfirst	snowflake
bookworm	daylight	downtown	(headlight)	snowstorm
cookbook	flashlight	downpour	headphones	snowplow
scrapbook	sunlight	countdown	headstrong	
	(headlight)			

Sort, Check, and Reflect

Have students shuffle their words and repeat the sort under your supervision. Ask students to identify the parts of words that might be hard to spell such as the *ache* in *headache* or the *weight* in *lightweight*. Have them check their sorts by looking for, or underlining, the word part that is shared by all the words in each column. Encourage the students to reflect and declare their understanding of what a compound word is.

Extend

Have students think of other words that share these same word parts. Some include: *bookkeeper, textbook, downstream, download, downcast, downfall, headband, headway, headline, snowdrift, snowshoe,* and *snowball*.

SORT 11   MORE COMPOUND WORDS

Demonstrate, Sort, Check, and Reflect

(See page 31.) This collection features compound words that are not so easy to define. Rather than ask students the meaning of the words, ask them to use them in sentences. Introduce this sort in a manner similar to Sort 10. Some words may be sorted in more than one place, as shown by those in parentheses below.

some**body**	him**self**	any**one**	every**thing**	with**out**	in**side**
(something)	themselves	everyone	anything*	outside	beside
sometime	yourself	(someone)	nothing	throughout	sideways
somewhere	herself		(something)	checkout	
somehow	myself*				
(someone)	itself				

*Among the top 300 high-frequency words

Extend

Have students think of other words that share these same word parts. Some include: *someday, plaything, blackout, blowout, cookout, hideout, outfit, checkout, timeout, outfield, outlaw, outlast, outline, outlive, everywhere, everyplace,* and *hillside*. Point out the plural of *self* in *themselves* to review that plural form. Ask students to look for any compound words they can find when doing a word hunt, rather than looking for more words with these same word parts.

SORT 10   Compound Words

bookcase	**ligh**thouse	**snow**man
headache	**down**hill	headphones
downstairs	headfirst	bookmark
snowflake	downtown	daylight
flashlight	bookworm	downpour
snowstorm	headlight	cookbook
scrapbook	sunlight	countdown
snowplow	headstrong	lightweight

SORT 11   More Compound Words

somebody	**himself**	**everything**
anyone	**without**	**inside**
something	itself	everyone
outside	anything	beside
sometime	yourself	throughout
sideways	herself	somewhere
nothing	somehow	someone
myself	checkout	themselves

Unit III   Syllable Juncture

NOTES FOR THE TEACHER

Background and Objectives

"Syllable juncture" is a term used to describe the point at which two syllables join. The pattern of vowels and consonants that meet at this point sends cues to the reader about the likely point of division that might be useful in decoding an unfamiliar word and the sound of the vowel in the first syllable. Learning about the patterns of vowels and consonants on either side of the syllable juncture helps spellers, too. For example, spellers will face decisions such as whether to put one or two consonants in the middle of a word (e.g., is it *dinner* or *diner*?). Knowledge of syllable juncture patterns is therefore a useful tool for analyzing the longer words readers and spellers will encounter.

A number of syllable patterns occur at the juncture. The ones that are covered in these five sorts include open and closed syllables and their variations: VCV, VCCV, VCCCV, VVCV, and VV. The other syllable types will be covered in the study of vowel patterns in stressed syllables that follows. The most reliable pattern of vowels and consonants is the VCCV pattern in words such as *supper* and *winter*. The VCCV pattern regularly signals that the first syllable is closed with a short-vowel sound. A variation of the VCCV pattern is the closed VCCCV pattern as in *tumble*.

The VCV pattern most often represents the open syllable with a long-vowel sound in the first syllable, as in *super* and *diner*, when the syllable is split after the long vowel (V/CV) and left "open." However, there are also many words in which the syllable division comes after the consonant (VC/V), as in *wag-on* where the first syllable has a short-vowel sound. Variations of the open-syllable pattern are the VVCV pattern in *reason* and the VV pattern in *create*. Although you can introduce and use the terms "open" and "closed" when referring to syllables, it might be best to focus on the pattern of vowels and consonants at the syllable juncture. You undoubtedly have intuitive knowledge about syllables, but you will learn along with your students as that knowledge is made explicit through these sorts. Students will:

- Identify the pattern where syllables join (VCV, VCCV, VV, etc.) and the point where syllables divide
- Identify the vowel sound in the first syllable
- Separate words into syllables
- Spell the words in these sorts correctly

Targeted Learners

These sorts are designed for students in the middle syllables and affixes stage who make errors at the point where syllables join. They may spell BOTEL for *bottle* or FAVVOR for *favor*, using but confusing the number of letters in the middle of two-syllable words. You may use Spell Check 2 on page 38 to assess this feature in more detail. Simply call out the words in a traditional test format without asking students to sort them into categories. Students who miss only one or two words can go on to other sorts.

Teaching Tips

The words selected for Sorts 12 to 16 are among the most frequent two-syllable words and should be easy to read by students in the early syllables and affixes stage. The words in Sort 15 are not as common, but this is a logical place to introduce and contrast the patterns. More words are suggested in the lists that follow most sorts and in the Appendix of *WTW*. You might use these lists to develop more sorts and sorts with more challenging words or you might ask students to apply what they have learned in the word sorts to read and spell these additional words.

Students should work with the words in these sorts for about a week using the standard weekly routines described on pages 6–7. During a word hunt, students should be able to find more words that fit the feature in just about any materials they are reading. The exception is the patterns in Sort 15 which are more rare.

Throughout this unit students will be thinking about how words are broken into syllables. They can be asked to indicate syllable division in their word study notebooks as they write the words (*su-per* or *su/per*) or you might ask them to cut apart their word cards at the syllable juncture.

The card game Match described in Chapter 5 of *WTW* and the Classic Card Game and Word Study Uno in Chapter 6 are games that can be adapted for syllable patterns. Card games are popular with students in the middle elementary grades and any game that has four to five categories can be adapted to review these syllable features.

SORT 12   SYLLABLE JUNCTURE IN VCV AND VCCV PATTERNS

Demonstrate

(See page 39.) You might introduce this lesson by asking your students to spell *super* and *supper*. Ask them to explain why they spelled the words as they did but do not tell them yourself. Assure them that the sort you are doing that week will help them understand what is going on with such words. Explain to your students that you will be looking at patterns in a different way and introduce the headers VCV and VCCV. Put the key words *super* and *supper* under the headers and explain how the letters in the headers refer only to the pattern of vowels and consonants in the middle of the word where two syllables come together. Underline the letters in the words and label them: VCV represents the *u*, *p*, and *e* in *super*, whereas VCCV represents the *u*, *p*, *p*, and *e* in *supper*. Notice that one or more letters, or no letters, can come on either side of the juncture. Sort several more words, then begin to involve your students in the sorting process by showing them a word and asking them where it should be placed. Continue with your students' help to sort all the words into columns under each header. For now the oddball *busy*, which has the pattern but not the long sound of *u*, should be sorted under VCV.

Next read down the VCV column of words and ask your students to listen to the vowel sound in the first syllable. They should notice that in each word the vowel sound is long except for the word *busy*. Move this word to the oddball category. Explain that these first syllables that end with a long-vowel sound are called "open." You might demonstrate how to break words into two syllables by cutting them apart or by drawing a line between the two syllables, as in *su/per*. Remind them that they have studied open syllables in words that end with a vowel such as *go, row,* and *blue*. Next, read the VCCV column to find that the vowel is short in the first syllable. Again you might cut apart the words or draw a line between the syllables (*sup/per*) and explain that these syllables are called "closed" because the short-vowel sound is "closed" with a consonant. Remind them of words such as *fled, drag, trip,* and *stop* that have the VC pattern. Your final sort will look something like the following:

VCV		VCCV		oddball
super	over*	**supper**	rabbit	busy
diner	ruler	dinner	kitten	
tiger	crazy	happy*	hello	
later	open*	pretty*	letter*	
paper	tiny	penny	lesson	
even		puppy	summer	

*Among the top 300 high-frequency words

Sort, Check, and Reflect

After modeling the sort have students repeat the sort with your guidance. To reinforce the idea of the syllables, you might ask them to draw a line between them or they could do this in their word study notebooks. Have them check their sorts by looking for the pattern in each column. Encourage the students to reflect by asking them how the words in each column are alike and what they have learned. Help the students to articulate a generalization such as, "A syllable that ends in a vowel usually has a long-vowel sound, and a syllable that ends in a consonant usually has a short-vowel sound."

Extend

Students should work with the words using some of the weekly routines. A word hunt will turn up many words as well as oddballs that will foreshadow other sorts to come. Have them put oddballs into a third column and keep them handy for further reference.

Additional Words.   *baby, bonus, basic, humid, tulip, pirate, robot, rodent, unit, zero, bottom, blizzard, fellow, hammer, mammal, muffin, puppet, sudden, slipper, tennis, guppy*

SORT 13   MORE SYLLABLE JUNCTURE IN VCV AND VCCV PATTERNS

(See page 40.) This sort reinforces the patterns from the previous sort, but adds VCC words that have different consonants at the juncture (*number*) to contrast with the words that have the same consonant at the juncture or "doublets" (*happen*). This sort can be introduced in a manner similar to Sort 12, or students can be asked to determine the categories for themselves in a student-centered sort. Students might go back to the word hunt from the last sort to find words that fit in this new category. *Water* and *only* are high-frequency oddballs. *Water* has a vowel sound that is neither the long nor the short sound for *a* and *only* has a long vowel in a VCCV pattern.

VCV	VCCV doublet	VCCV different	oddball
silent	**happen**	**number***	water*
female	better*	winter	only*
fever	follow	problem	
moment	funny*	after*	
	yellow*	finger	
	pattern	sister*	
	bottom	chapter	
	pillow	member	
		blanket	
		window	

*Among the top 300 high-frequency words

Additional Words. *crater, crisis, duty, hero, navy, siren, vacant, blossom, dipper, gallop, butter, matter, hollow, tunnel, valley, basket, center, cactus, dentist, goblet, helmet, insect, kidnap, magnet, master, seldom, tablet, temper, trumpet, basket, wonder*

SORT 14   SYLLABLE JUNCTURE IN VCV AND VVCV PATTERNS

Demonstrate, Sort, Check, and Reflect

(See page 41.) The VCV pattern is most often the open syllable with a long-vowel sound as in *hu-man*, but there are also many words in which VCV has a closed syllable, as in *nev-er*. Explain how the headers V/CV and VC/V indicate this. The VVCV juncture pattern is a variation of the open-syllable pattern because the syllable still ends with a vowel that has the long-vowel sound. Introduce this sort in a way similar to Sorts 12 and 13. Ask students to revisit earlier word hunts to find words that might fit the new categories established here. Speculate about why the letter *v* might not be doubled in words such as *river, never,* and *seven*. Write these words with a double *v* and notice how the two *vs* begin to look like a *w*. The letter *v* never doubles (*savvy* and *revved* are exceptions).

V/CV (long)		VC/V (short)		VVCV (long)
human	music	**never***	finish	**reason**
pilot		river	seven*	meeting
frozen		visit	present*	peanut
student		wagon	second*	leader
humor		planet	minute	sneaker
lazy		lemon		easy

*Among the top 300 high-frequency words

Extend

Use the VCV words in the alternative words to prepare a list for students to read (or write them in sentences like: *I saw a comet last night.*). Have them practice using both a short vowel and a long vowel to read the word as a way to practice the flexible decoding strategy needed when reading words with the VCV pattern. (Is the word *co-met* or *com-et*?) They should check the pronunciation against what makes sense or whether they have heard the word before.

Additional Words.   *famous, labor, legal, private, recent, spiral, ozone, stupid, chapel, city, comet, credit, critic, denim, dozen, devil, limit, lizard, melon, panel, prison, wizard, waiter, season, eagle, diary, shovel*

SORT 15   SYLLABLE JUNCTURE IN VCCCV AND VV PATTERNS

(See page 42.) The VV juncture pattern represents a variation of the open syllable with a juncture between the two vowels and a long vowel in the first syllable. The VCCCV pattern is a variation of the closed syllable with the split between syllables coming before or after a consonant blend or digraph (*pil-grim, ath-lete*).

Demonstrate, Sort, Check, and Reflect

Introduce this sort with either a teacher-directed, guess my category, or student-centered sort. In a word hunt it will be hard for students to find many more VV words but challenge them to try. There are many VCCCV words that end in *-le* (*settle,* for example) that can be added in a word hunt. The study of words that end in *-le* is explored more in Sorts 29 and 30, but would not be out of place here.

VCC/CV		VC/CCV		V/V	
athlete	mushroom	**pilgrim**	hundred	**create**	cruel
kingdom		complete	inspect	poet	lion
pumpkin		monster	children	riot	diet
halfway		kitchen		duet	poem
English		control		trial	giant

Additional Words.   *actress, address, enchant, congress, laughter, paddle, settle, sandwich, constant, complain, instant, merchant, ostrich, orchard, orphan, purchase, subtract, boa, bias, fuel, chaos, liar, neon, trio, idea, violin, area*

SORT 16   OPEN AND CLOSED SYLLABLES AND INFLECTED ENDINGS

Demonstrate, Sort, Check, and Reflect

(See page 43.) This extra sort is designed to help students see the relationship between the rules they learned for inflected endings and the syllable juncture patterns they have been studying in this unit. It reviews the inflected rules covered in Sorts 1 to 5.

Put up the syllable juncture headings and ask students to sort the words as they have been doing for Sorts 12 to 15. Ask them what they notice about the words in the first column. What rule did they learn about adding *-ed* and *-ing* to words like these? Repeat this with each column, helping students see how the rules for adding these inflected endings honor the syllable juncture patterns they have been studying. Pose questions such as: *If we did not double the* p *in* hopping, *how would we be likely to read that word?* (hoping) *Why?* (The first syllable would look open because it would not clearly end with a consonant.) *Why don't we double the last letter in a word like* acted? (The syllable is already closed and ends with a consonant.) A second sort could be done under the headers of "*e*-drop," "double," and "nothing" to review the rules. In that sort *painted, panting, telling*, and *hunted* would be separated from words that double.

VCV	VCCV	VVCV	e-drop	double	nothing
hoping	**hopping**	**cleaned**	hoping	hopping	cleaned
quoted	plotting	leaking	quoted	plotting	panting
faded	wrapped	greeted	faded	wrapped	greeted
racing	nodded	shouting	racing	winning	shouting
skated	painted	floated	skated	nodded	floated
saving	panting	needed	saving	letting	needed
joking	winning		joking	skipped	leaking
	hunted				painted
	telling				telling
	letting				hunted
	skipped				

Extend

Give students base words like *doze, hire, test, skim, point, hate, scan*, etc., and ask them to add both *-ed* and *-ing* to them, applying the rules reviewed in this sort.

Additional Words.   *dozing, hiring, noted, posing, rated, drafted, linking, shifted, testing, skimming, scanning, braided, cheated, heating, pointing*

SPELL CHECK 2   ASSESSMENT FOR SYLLABLE JUNCTURE PATTERNS

Call out the words below for students to spell. All of these words have appeared in previous sorts.

1. summer	**2.** easy	**3.** finish	**4.** poet
5. leader	**6.** lion	**7.** river	**8.** hundred
9. never	**10.** complete	**11.** reason	**12.** English
13. giant	**14.** lazy	**15.** saving	**16.** tiger
17. moment	**18.** number	**19.** sister	**20.** waited

To review all the syllable juncture patterns you may want to ask students to write the word in the appropriate category as shown below. Tell them to think about the letters in the middle of the words as you call them aloud. Then write each word under the heading that shows the pattern of letters in the middle. This form can be found on page 44.

VCCV	VCCCV	VC/V first syllable short
summer	English	river
number	hundred	finish
sister	complete	never

V/CV first syllable long	VVCV	VV
tiger	reason	lion
moment	easy	giant
lazy	leader	poet
saving	waited	

SORT 12   Syllable Jun_cture in VCV and VCCV Patterns

VCV	VCCV	*oddball*
super	**supper**	diner
dinner	tiger	happy
later	busy	pretty
paper	penny	even
tiny	over	puppy
rabbit	ruler	kitten
hello	crazy	letter
lesson	summer	open

SORT 13   More Syllable Juncture in VCV and VCCV Patterns

VCV	VCCV doublet	VCCV different	*oddball*
silent	**happen**		**number**
funny	winter		follow
female	better		problem
after	moment		pattern
sister	finger		bottom
chapter	fever		member
blanket	pillow		water
only	yellow		window

SORT 14   Syllable Juncture in VCV and VVCV Patterns

V/CV long	VC/V short	VVCV long
human	**never**	**reason**
river	pilot	visit
meeting	wagon	planet
lemon	frozen	peanut
finish	student	seven
leader	lazy	present
easy	second	music
sneaker	humor	minute

SORT 15   Syllable Junctures in VCCCV and VV Patterns

VCC/CV	VC/CCV	V/V
athlete	**pilgrim**	**create**
control	complete	children
poet	duet	pumpkin
monster	riot	mushroom
halfway	kitchen	trial
poem	English	hundred
cruel	giant	lion
kingdom	inspect	diet

SORT 16   Open and Closed Syllables and Inflected Endings

VCV	VCCV	VVCV
hoping	**hopping**	**cleaned**
skipped	plotting	quoted
joking	wrapped	greeted
telling	winning	hunted
racing	nodded	shouting
skated	panting	floated
leaking	letting	needed
saving	painted	faded

Spell Check 2   Assessment for Syllable Juncture Patterns

Name _____

Directions: Listen to the word your teacher calls aloud. Think of the letters in the middle of the word. Write the word under the heading that shows the pattern of letters.

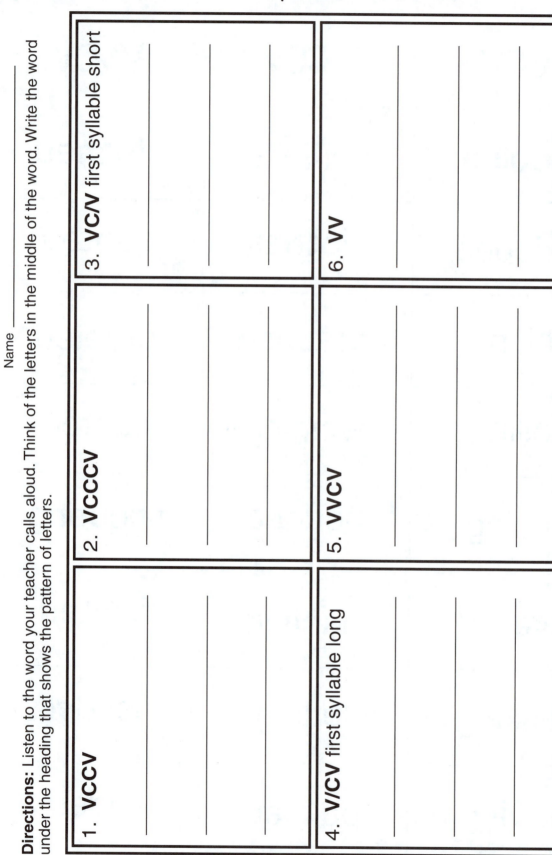

1. VCCV

2. VCCCV

3. VC/V first syllable short

4. V/CV first syllable long

5. VVCV

6. VV

Unit IV Vowel Patterns in Accented Syllables

NOTES FOR THE TEACHER

Background and Objectives

The vowel patterns studied in the within word pattern stage reappear in two-syllable words in these sorts. For example, the *ai* pattern in *rain* is also in *painter* and *complain*. In these sorts students will revisit common vowel patterns and then less common vowel patterns. Because there are so many of these patterns this is a large unit containing 11 different sorts. It has been divided into two parts with Spell Check 3 following Sort 21 to review the long-vowel patterns and Spell Check 4 following Sort 28 to review the other vowel patterns. Students will also be introduced to the notion of accent or stress (we use these terms interchangeably) and helped to see that the vowel sound is clearly heard in the accented syllable. Sometimes students can "feel" the stress if they gently place the top of their hand or their thumb under their chin as they say the words.

Accent or stress may vary with regional dialects. Do you say **rac**coon or rac**coon**? Students may disagree at times about which syllable is stressed, and you may disagree with our categories as well. The dictionary can be consulted as the final arbiter. However, there is no reason to focus on right or wrong answers, and ambiguous words can simply go into the oddball category if desired. Many students will struggle to identify stressed syllables, but do not be overly concerned about this. Being able to identify the stressed syllable is not the primary goal in these sorts. Stress is simply one more way to understand the regularity of the spelling system and how vowel sounds and vowel patterns are fairly reliable in stressed syllables. Some understanding of syllable stress will help students try alternative pronunciations when attempting to sound out an unfamiliar word or understand how to use the pronunciation guide for words they look up in the dictionary. It will also help ELLs learning to pronounce English. Students will:

- Identify accented syllables and familiar vowel patterns
- Spell the words in these sorts

Targeted Learners

These sorts are for students in the middle syllables and affixes stage of spelling who can spell single-syllable vowel patterns correctly for the most part but make mistakes in two-syllable words. They might spell *serving* as SURVING or *shower* as SHOUER. Many students will benefit from this review of vowel patterns. Students who have not learned to identify and use vowel patterns in earlier grades can learn that now in the context of these more difficult words. Use Spell Checks 3 and 4 as pretests (pages 50 and 55) to

45

determine more accurately which students need work on these words. Students who score 90% or better can move on to other features.

Teaching Tips

See the standard weekly routines listed on pages 6–7 to engage your students in repeated practice and extensions. Throughout this unit students will be thinking about where accent falls as well as how words are broken into syllables. They can be asked to indicate syllable division and syllable stress in their word study notebooks: <u>brace</u> let, a <u>wake</u>. Once words are sorted by the syllable that contains the vowel pattern, it is much easier to identify stressed syllables.

Keep dictionaries handy and encourage their use when questions arise. Some of the words in these sorts and the ones to follow will not be as well known, and students should be encouraged to look up the meanings of words to add to the introductory discussion for each sort. Some suggestions are given in the sorts that follow about the use of the dictionary for specific features.

Students will see some familiar base words in many of these words (e.g., *painter*, *delight*, *lightning*). Point these out and talk about how they will be easier to spell when the base word is identified. Sometimes you may ask students to identify verbs and add *-ing*, *-ed*, or *-s* to review the rules introduced in earlier sorts. You may also ask students to identify nouns and write the plural forms. These can be written in their word study notebooks. At other times you may review compound words or syllable juncture patterns.

When students go on word hunts for vowel sounds, welcome single-syllable words as well as two-syllable words, because they will confirm that the same patterns are used to spell the sounds. Finding additional words with these same patterns may be challenging for students, so do not hold them accountable for finding any certain number of them in a word hunt. Instead you may want to focus on creating class lists that are added to throughout the unit.

Games from Chapter 6 of *WTW* that feature vowel patterns should work here. Stressbusters, a game described in Chapter 7, can be used throughout this unit with different words each week.

SORT 17   LONG -*A* PATTERNS IN ACCENTED SYLLABLES

Demonstrate

(See page 56.) Read the words aloud and discuss any that might be unfamiliar such as *pavement* or *decay*. Ask your students what they notice about this collection of words. They should notice that all the words have the long sound of *a*. Put up the three headers and key words. Point out that the long -*a* sound is in the first syllable of *rainbow* and in the second syllable of *awake*. Sort the rest of the words with the students' help. *Chocolate* and *again* should go into the oddball column because they do not have the sound of long -*a* even though the last syllable has a long -*a* pattern. When all the words have been sorted, read down each column, stressing the first syllable slightly. Explain to students that the first syllable in each word is stressed or accented, and that when we say those words we put a little more emphasis on the first syllable. Have them read the words with you. Sometimes students can "feel" the stress if they gently place the top of their hand under their chin as they say the words. Repeat this with the second column where the stress is on the second syllable. The first sort will look something like the following:

1st		2nd		oddball
rainbow	bracelet	**awake**	amaze	chocolate
painter	pavement	contain	today*	again*
raisin	basement	complain	explain	
crayon	payment	decay	remain	
mayor		mistake	obey	
maybe		parade		
		escape		

*Among the top 300 high-frequency words

During this same introductory lesson or on another day, ask students if they can think of another way to sort these words. Someone perhaps will mention the different patterns of long -a. Set up _rainbow, awake_, and _crayon_ as headers and underline the spelling in each accented syllable. Sort the rest of the words with the students' help into one of these three categories. _Obey_ will be an oddball because it has the sound of long -a but not one of the patterns. _Chocolate_ and _again_ have the pattern but not the sound. The pattern sort will look something like the following:

<u>rai</u>nbow	aw<u>ake</u>	cr<u>ay</u>on	oddball
painter	bracelet	mayor	again*
raisin	pavement	maybe	chocolate
contain	mistake	decay	obey
complain	parade	today*	
remain	amaze	payment	
explain	basement		
	escape		

*High-frequency word

Sort, Check, and Reflect

After modeling each sort have students repeat the sorts (both by syllable stress and vowel patterns) under your supervision. Have them check their sorts by looking for the pattern in each column. In these sorts students can tell where the accented syllable is by where the long -a pattern is. Encourage the students to reflect by asking them how the words in each column are alike and what they have learned.

Extend

Students should work with the words using the standard weekly routines on pages 6–7. During a word hunt they will find words with the long -a pattern that are not stressed such as _locate, essay_, or _dictate_. These words can still be added to the pattern sorts.

You may want to have students look up some of the words in a dictionary to see how accent or stress is indicated in the pronunciation guide. Dictionaries differ. Some may use accent marks and others use bold lettering. Students might then be asked to break their words into syllables and indicate the accented syllables with an accent mark or by underlining. This can become a new routine to do throughout this unit in their word study notebooks. Ask students to add -ing and -ed to verbs such as _decay_ (_decayed, decaying_), _obey_ (_obeyed, obeying_) _escape_ (_escaped, escaping_), _remain_ (_remained, remaining_), and _explain_ (_explained, explaining_)

Additional Words.   _daisy, dainty, trainer, straighten, sprained, railroad, grateful, baseball, basement, prayer, player, vibrate, crusade, insane, embrace, dismay, delay, sustain, exclaim, refrain, terrain, regain, hooray, betray,_ oddballs: _captain, bargain, garbage_

SORT 18   LONG -*I* PATTERNS IN ACCENTED SYLLABLES

Demonstrate, Sort, Check, and Reflect

(See page 57.) Introduce the sort in a manner similar to Sort 17; that is, sort by the syllable containing the long -*i* sound. Sort the words a second time by the pattern for long -*i* using *frighten* and *polite* as headers. Underline the spelling of long -*i* to focus attention on the specific pattern. *Machine, forgive,* and *favorite* are oddballs that have familiar long -*i* patterns but do not have the long -*i* sound.

1st		2nd		oddball
frighten	sidewalk	**beside**	combine	machine
ninety	highway	delight	arrive	forgive
higher	brightly	surprise	provide	favorite
driveway		decide	invite	
slightly		advice	describe	
lightning		survive	polite	

Additional Words.   *lively, nightmare, tighten, divide, excite, confide, recline, tonight, recite, collide, advise, ignite, despite, divine, resign, design*

Words with the open syllable could be added as well: *visor, minus, item, Friday, icy, climax, trial, client, dial,* and *rival.*

Extend

Have students identify the compound words (*forgive, sidewalk, driveway, highway*) and then challenge them to find or think of other words that form compounds with *way* (*fairway, wayward, wayside,* etc.). Ask students to find words that contain a base word (e.g., *ninety*). Talk about the difference between compounds and base words (base words have an ending that cannot stand alone as a word).

SORT 19   LONG -*O* PATTERNS IN ACCENTED SYLLABLES

(See page 58.) Introduce the sort in a manner similar to Sort 17; that is, sort by the syllable containing the long -*o* sound. You may want to try a student-centered or guess my category sort as an alternative by removing the headers. Sort again by the patterns for long -*o* using *below, hostess, explode,* and *toaster* as headers. *Europe* is an oddball that does not have the sound of long -*o*. Ask students to find three words that have the same base word (*lonely, lonesome,* and *alone*). Talk about how they are related in meaning.

Sort by Accented Syllable

1st		2nd		oddball
toaster	poster	**below**	approach	Europe
hostess	soapy	explode	awoke	
lonely	bowling	suppose	erode	
owner	soldier	compose		
lower	postage	decode		
lonesome	coaster	remote		
loafer		alone		

Sort by Vowel Patterns

to*aster*	be*low*	ex*plode*	*hostess*	oddball
loafer	owner	lonely	postage	Europe
soapy	lower	lonesome	soldier	
approach	bowling	erode	poster	
coaster		suppose		
		compose		
		decode		
		remote		
		alone		
		awoke		

Additional Words. *hopeful, closely, coastal, rowboat, mower, molding, oatmeal, enclose, disown, enroll, behold, revolt, tadpole, expose, oppose, console,* oddball: *bureau*

Words with the open syllable could be contrasted as well: *pony, chosen, donate, notice, sofa, frozen, soda, potion, rotate, stolen,* and *cocoa*.

SORT 20   LONG -*U* PATTERNS IN ACCENTED SYLLABLES

(See page 59.) Introduce the sort in a manner similar to Sort 17; that is, sort by the syllable containing the long -*u* sound. You may want to try a student-centered or guess my category sort. Students will be familiar by now with the kinds of categories. Sort again by the pattern for long -*u*. In a vowel pattern sort, the following words will be oddballs: *Tuesday, beauty,* and *cougar*.

1st	2nd		Sort by Vowel Pattern		
rooster	**include**	*jew*el	**rooster**	in*clude*	**oddball**
Tuesday	refuse	fewer	cocoon	useful	Tuesday
useful	amuse	chewy	doodle	refuse	beauty
jewel	confuse		toothache	amuse	cougar
doodle	cocoon		noodle	confuse	
toothache	excuse		scooter	excuse	
noodle	pollute		balloon	pollute	
scooter	reduce		cartoon	reduce	
beauty	balloon		raccoon		
cougar	cartoon		shampoo		
fewer	raccoon				
chewy	shampoo				

Additional Words. *sewer, steward, pewter, moody, spoonful, foolish, poodle, lagoon, baboon, tattoo, maroon, conclude, perfume, consume, compute, exclude, salute, dispute, abuse, excuse*

Words with the open syllable: *pupil, rumor, tutor, ruler, July, fluid, dual, duet, fluent*

SORT 21   LONG -*E* PATTERNS IN ACCENTED SYLLABLES

(See page 60.) This sort is a little different because it includes the short sound of *e* (spelled *ea* as in *feather*) as well as the long sound. Ask students what they notice about the words for this week. They may have many ideas, such as that the words have both long and short -e sounds, which is different from the sorts they have been doing before this. Set up three headers and sort the words with the students' help, making sure that they attend to the sound of the vowel as well as to where the stressed pattern lies. Help students see that the same principles apply: In the stressed syllable we can clearly hear the vowel sound whether it is long or short. Sort again by both pattern and sound as shown in the second sort below. There are plenty of words for a second sort listed under Additional Words. Just fill in the template in the Appendix.

Sort by Long or Short Sound in Accented Syllable

1st long		1st short		2nd long	
needle	meaning	**feather**	steady	**succeed**	extreme
season	eastern	leather	healthy	increase	fifteen
reader	people	heavy		compete	thirteen
feature		pleasant		defeat	repeat
freedom		sweater		indeed	

Sort by Pattern and Sound

needle	compete	season	feather	oddball
succeed	extreme	defeat	leather	people*
fifteen		repeat	heavy	
thirteen		meaning	pleasant	
indeed		eastern	sweater	
freedom		reader	steady	
		increase	healthy	
		feature		

*Among the top 300 high-frequency words

Additional Words. *freezer, breezy, cheetah, steeple, tweezers, beetle, feeble, greedy, sweeten, beaver, easel, reason, feature, creature, treaty, eagle, eager, cleaner, canteen, agree, degree, between, complete, supreme, athlete, trapeze, stampede, conceal, ideal, ready, steady, weather, sweaty, jealous, weapon, heaven, meadow, breakfast, instead*

Words with the open syllable could be contrasted as well: *zebra, meter, veto, prefix, tepee, decent, evil,* and *even*.

SPELL CHECK 3   ASSESSMENT FOR LONG-VOWEL PATTERNS IN ACCENTED SYLLABLES

The words below have been selected from previous lessons. Call them aloud for students to spell on a sheet of notebook paper. You can also ask students to rewrite them into categories and explain why they grouped them together. They might group by VV (*soapy, freedom*), Ve (*refuse, advice*), VC (*owner, payment*), and VCC (*highway, poster*).

1. complain	**2.** soapy	**3.** season	**4.** Tuesday
5. fifteen	**6.** owner	**7.** highway	**8.** awake
9. explode	**10.** freedom	**11.** refuse	**12.** balloon
13. invite	**14.** sweater	**15.** poster	**16.** payment
17. advice	**18.** compete	**19.** eastern	**20.** scooter

SORT 22   AMBIGUOUS VOWELS IN ACCENTED SYLLABLES (*OY/OI* AND *OU/OW*)

(See page 61.) Now we move into the study of vowels that are neither long nor short, or what we call ambiguous vowels. These include vowel digraphs, diphthongs, and *r*-controlled vowels in the accented syllable of two-syllable words.

Demonstrate, Sort, Check, and Reflect

Discuss the meaning of any words you think your students might not know. The word *counter* has several meanings and the difference between *county* and *country* might not be clear. Begin sorting words by accent using the headers **1st** and **2nd** to indicate which syllable is stressed. Then ask your students about the sound in the accented syllables under each header. Three different vowel sounds are included under the first header and two under the second. Set up these categories with the key words and then sort the rest of the words with student help as shown in the table below. A second sort by sound as well as pattern can follow, on another day if necessary. Use the key words as headers and underline the vowel pattern.

Accent and Sound Sort

1st				2nd	
voyage	**drowsy**	**country**		**destroy**	**about***
moisture	county	trouble		appoint	allow
loyal	counter	double		avoid	amount
poison	thousand	southern		annoy	around*
noisy	coward			employ	
	powder				

*Among the top 300 high-frequency words

Pattern Sort

voyage	**moisture**	**drowsy**	**about***	**country**
annoy	poison	allow	county	trouble
loyal	noisy	coward	counter	double
employ	appoint	powder	thousand	southern
destroy	avoid		amount	
			around	

*Among the top 300 high-frequency words

Extend

Send students on a word hunt to find more words that will fit into these categories. Welcome single-syllable words as well because they will confirm that the same patterns are showing up.

   The game of Oygo, described in Chapter 7 of *WTW*, and its variation Owgo can be used to reinforce the spellings of these words. There are plenty of words for another week of work on these patterns. Use the template in the Appendix and the words below.

Additional Words.   *joyful, royal, oyster, boycott, soybean, enjoy, ahoy, toilet, ointment, pointed, exploit, rejoice, turmoil, turquoise, prowler, tower, brownie, rowdy, shower, trowel, council, lousy, scoundrel, bounty, voucher, trousers, profound, surround, announce, youngster*

SORT 23   MORE AMBIGUOUS VOWELS IN ACCENTED SYLLABLES (*AU*, *AW*, *AL*)

(See page 62.) Discuss any word meanings that you think your students might not know, such as *gnawed*, *gawking*, or *flawless*. These words all share the same sound in the first accented syllable, so there is no sort by accent. Instead the headers call attention to the different patterns that spell the sound. Start the sort by asking students how the words are all alike. Introduce the headers and key words and sort the rest of the words with the students' help. *All right* is included because students often misspell this as *alright*, making it into a compound word when it should not be. *Laughed* has the *au* pattern but does not have the sound. Because these words are already sorted by pattern there is no second sort to do.

au	aw	al	oddball
saucer	**awful**	**also***	laughed
author	awkward	always*	all right
August	lawyer	almost	
autumn	awesome	although	
laundry	gnawed	already	
caution	gawking		
faucet	flawless		
sausage			
auction			
haunted			

*Among the top 300 high-frequency words

Additional Words.   *cauldron, gaudy, jaunty, haunches, trauma, pauper, cautious, awfully, drawing, lawless, tawny, yawning, brawny, walrus, walnut, altar, halter, salty, calmly, falter, waltz* oddballs: *drawer, wallet*

SORT 24   R-INFLUENCED A IN ACCENTED SYLLABLES

Demonstrate, Sort, Check, and Reflect

(See page 63.) This sort reviews two sounds associated with *r*-influenced *a*. The sound in the first syllable of *airplane* and the second syllable of *compare* is sometimes referred to as long, whereas the vowel sound in the first syllable of *garden* is referred to as short. Begin this sort by asking students about any words whose meaning they might not know (*declare* or *despair*, perhaps) and then ask how the words are all the same. This can be done as a student-centered sort by removing the headers before giving the students the words to sort. *Toward* is an oddball that anticipates the further study of words that begin with *w* in Sort 26. These words can be sorted again by pattern focusing upon the *air* in *airplane* and the *are* in *compare*.

1st *ar*	1st long -*a*	2nd long -*a*	oddball
garden	**airplane**	**compare**	toward
market	parents	aware	
carpet	haircut	despair	
harvest	dairy	repair	
marble	carry*	declare	
hardly	careful	beware	
partner	barely		
pardon	fairy		
barber			

*High-frequency word

Extend

Ask students to identify the compound word (*airplane*) and challenge them to brainstorm more compounds for *air* (*airmail, airport, airwaves, airline, aircraft*) and *hair* (*hairpin, hairbrush*). Ask students if *carpet* is a compound word. Why or why not?

Additional Words.   *artist, party, tardy, parka, larva, garlic, margin, bargain, carbon, scarlet, sparkle, target, harbor, carton, barefoot, stairway, fairway, airport, chairman, prairie, unfair, impair, affair, prepare, airfare, hardware, nightmare, software,* oddball: *lizard*

SORT 25   R-INFLUENCED O IN ACCENTED SYLLABLES

(See page 64.) Some discussion of word meanings may be needed with terms such as *ashore* or *corncob*. In these words the *r*-influenced sound of /or/ is spelled two ways (*or* and *ore*). Sort these words according to whether the stressed /or/ sound is heard in the first or second syllable. A second sort of words can separate out the ones that are spelled with *-ore. Sorry* is an oddball that has the pattern but an unexpected sound. *Reward* anticipates the next sort. You might draw students' attention to the first sound in *chorus*, which has the sound of hard *c* rather than the more familiar /ch/. (During the derivational relations stage, students will learn that this is a common letter-sound correspondence in Greek words that come from Greek.)

1st			2nd		oddball
morning *	forty	stormy	**before** *	ignore	sorry
shorter	northern		record	adore	reward
order*	border		perform	inform	
forest	corncob		ashore		
corner	chorus		report		
normal	florist		explore		

*Among the top 300 high-frequency words

Additional Words.   *torment, fortress, tortoise, portrait, boring, orchard, horrid, hornet, normal, forward, organ, morsel, orbit, restore, galore, afford, reform, distort, endorse, import*

SORT 26   WORDS WITH THE W OR /W/ SOUND BEFORE THE VOWEL

(See page 65.) Like *r, w* (or *u* when it has the /w/ sound as in *quarter*) can influence the vowel. In these words the sound of *w* exerts an influence on the vowel that follows it, changing the *ar* in *warmth* to sound like /or/ and the *or* in *worker* to a sound like /er/. What would normally be a short *-a* in a CVC word like *watch* is the broad *-a* sound. In these words the focus is only on the first syllable. Discuss the meanings of words such as *squabble* that might not be familiar to your students. *Wardrobe* might be related to the book and movie, *The Lion, the Witch, and the Wardrobe,* by C. S. Lewis. Students should be able to sort these words with little direction, but do spend time reflecting on what the sorts reveal. Help the students form generalizations about how *w* works in these words.

It may be difficult to find more words with these patterns and sounds in word hunts. Students can look for other words that begin with *w* (such as *window* or *weekend*) in which the vowel after the *w* is not influenced by it. This will help them see that this influence is limited to words that begin with *wa* or *wo*. Help them recall the words *toward* and *reward* from previous sorts and have them add these words to their word study notebook under other *war* words to see that they are no longer oddballs. Remember that students may not always agree about the exact sound in a word because of variations in dialect. This is especially true of *r*-influenced vowels, so be ready to accept these differences and let students sort by their own dialect.

war		wor		wa	
warmth	quarter	**worker**	worship	**watch**	squabble
wardrobe	quarrel	worse	worthwhile	waffle	squad
warning	swarm	world		wander	
warden	dwarf	worry		squat	
warrior	backward	worthy		squash	

Additional Words.   *squalid, swaddle, swallow, waddle, wallow, wallet, water*

SORT 27   SCHWA + *R* SPELLED *ER*, *IR*, AND *UR* IN FIRST SYLLABLES

(See page 66.) In these words the same *r*-influenced vowel sound in the first syllable is spelled three different ways, so you can introduce this sort in a manner similar to Sort 23. *Spirit* and *every* are oddballs because they have the spelling pattern, but not the sound of the words in this sort.

er	ir	ur	oddball
nervous	**thirty**	**sturdy**	spirit
person	firmly	purpose	every*
perfect	dirty	further	
certain	birthday	hurry	
mermaid	thirsty	purple	
perhaps	birdbath	turtle	
service		furnish	
		during	
		Thursday	

*Among the top 300 high-frequency words

Additional Words.   *gerbil, merchant, version, servant, persist, verdict, circus, virtue, twirler, skirmish, circuit, irksome, whirlpool, chirping, burger, mural, surfer, burden, curfew, hurdle, jury, murmur, turnip, burner, murder, surplus*

SORT 28   SCHWA + *R* AND *R*-INFLUENCED *E* IN ACCENTED SYLLABLES (*ER*, *EAR*, *ERE*)

(See page 67.) This is a somewhat complicated sort that you should introduce as teacher directed. Begin with a sound sort using just two headers to represent the two sounds: *er* (/ ər/ or /ur/) and *ear/ere/eer* (/ēr/). After sorting by the sound in the accented syllable, ask your students what they notice about the spellings in each column (the / ər/ sound is spelled with both *er* and *ear*). Use the key words to establish subcategories and sort the words by pattern so that the final sort looks something like the following:

er = /ur/	ear = /ur/	ear/ere/eer		
mercy	**early***	**nearby**	**severe**	**career**
sermon	earthquake	teardrop	sincere	cheerful
serpent	learner	spearmint	adhere	
hermit	pearly	yearbook	merely	
thermos	rehearse	appear		
kernel	yearn	dreary		

*Among the top 300 high-frequency words

Additional Words.   *earnings, earthworm, earnest, yearning, research, clearing, dearest, earache, eerie, bleary, weary, nearly, revere, endear*

SPELL CHECK 4   ASSESSMENT FOR *R*-INFLUENCED AND AMBIGUOUS VOWELS IN ACCENTED SYLLABLES

Retention Test

The words below have been selected from previous lessons. Call them aloud for students to spell on a sheet of notebook paper and then ask the students to rewrite them into categories and explain why they grouped them together.

1. noisy	**2.** autumn	**3.** marble	**4.** forest
5. quarter	**6.** person	**7.** nearby	**8.** thousand
9. before	**10.** awful	**11.** repair	**12.** amount
13. sincere	**14.** worry	**15.** thirty	**16.** early
17. Thursday	**18.** destroy	**19.** always	**20.** rarely

SORT 17   Long -*a* Patterns in Accented Syllables

1st	2nd	*oddball*
rainbow	**awake**	painter
contain	obey	raisin
complain	decay	crayon
mistake	chocolate	parade
mayor	maybe	basement
escape	bracelet	amaze
again	today	pavement
explain	payment	remain

SORT 18   Long -*i* Patterns in Accented Syllables

1st	2nd	*oddball*
frighten	**beside**	surprise
decide	advice	machine
survive	driveway	combine
forgive	provide	slightly
ninety	invite	favorite
describe	lightning	polite
sidewalk	higher	brightly
delight	arrive	highway

SORT 19   Long -o Patterns in Accented Syllables

1st	2nd	*oddball*
toaster	**below**	coaster
alone	hostess	explode
soldier	suppose	lonely
compose	owner	decode
lower	remote	lonesome
approach	loafer	awoke
postage	soapy	Europe
bowling	erode	poster

SORT 20   Long -*u* Patterns in Accented Syllables

1ˢᵗ	2ⁿᵈ	*oddball*
rooster	**include**	Tuesday
reduce	balloon	useful
cartoon	doodle	fewer
jewel	refuse	raccoon
toothache	excuse	noodle
beauty	shampoo	pollute
chewy	scooter	confuse
cocoon	cougar	amuse

SORT 21   Long -*e* Patterns in Accented Syllables

1ˢᵗ long	1ˢᵗ short	2ⁿᵈ long
needle	**feather**	**succeed**
season	increase	leather
compete	repeat	defeat
feature	heavy	freedom
pleasant	meaning	indeed
extreme	fifteen	sweater
eastern	steady	healthy
people	reader	thirteen

SORT 22   Ambiguous Vowels in Accented Syllables (*oy/oi* and *ou/ow*)

1st	2nd	
voyage	**about**	**drowsy**
destroy	**country**	moisture
coward	amount	thousand
avoid	poison	trouble
noisy	annoy	employ
allow	double	loyal
county	around	powder
appoint	counter	southern

SORT 23   More Ambiguous Vowels in Accented Syllables (*au, aw, al*)

au	*aw*	*al*
saucer	**awful**	**also**
always	author	almost
August	all right	lawyer
although	awkward	autumn
laundry	laughed	awesome
gnawed	caution	flawless
faucet	already	auction
gawking	sausage	haunted

SORT 24   *r*-Influenced *a* in Accented Syllables

1ˢᵗ *ar*	1ˢᵗ long -*a*	2ⁿᵈ long -*a*
garden	airplane	compare
careful	market	aware
carpet	despair	parents
toward	haircut	harvest
marble	repair	carry
fairy	hardly	declare
partner	beware	pardon
barber	barely	dairy

SORT 25   *r*-Influenced *o* in Accented Syllables

1st	2nd	*oddball*
morning	**before**	order
record	shorter	perform
forest	sorry	normal
reward	corner	ashore
forty	report	northern
explore	border	stormy
corncob	chorus	ignore
adore	florist	inform

SORT 26   Words with the w or /w/ Sound Before the Vowel

war	*wor*	*wa*
warmth	**worker**	**watch**
quarter	wardrobe	worse
world	waffle	warden
warning	worry	squad
squat	warrior	worthy
quarrel	worship	swarm
worthwhile	dwarf	squabble
squash	wander	backward

SORT 27   Schwa + *r* Spelled *er*, *ir*, and *ur* in First Syllables

er	*ir*	*ur*	*oddball*
nervous	**thirty**	**sturdy**	
firmly	person	purpose	
perfect	further	dirty	
hurry	birthday	certain	
spirit	mermaid	Thursday	
perhaps	turtle	thirsty	
birdbath	service	furnish	
during	every	purple	

SORT 28   Schwa + *r* and *r*-Influenced *e* in Accented Syllables (*er*, *ear*, *ere*)

er = /ur/	*ear* = /ur/	*ear* /*ere* /*eer*
mercy	early	nearby
career	severe	earthquake
spearmint	sermon	teardrop
kernel	pearly	yearbook
sincere	hermit	learner
rehearse	appear	thermos
adhere	dreary	cheerful
yearn	serpent	merely

Unit V   Unaccented Syllables

NOTES FOR THE TEACHER

Background and Objectives

In previous sorts, the feature of attention was familiar vowel patterns in the accented syllable. Now we turn our attention to the unaccented syllable in which the sound is often the *schwa* sound /ə/, as in the first syllable of *about*, or the final sound in *table* or *nickel*. These unaccented syllables are challenging to spell because the same sound is spelled several different ways (Is it *nickel, nickle,* or *nickil*?) and sound is not a useful clue. Although generalizations sometimes govern which spelling is used, students must also memorize which spelling goes with a particular word, and repeated sorts will help them do this. As these sorts will show, however, some spellings are much more likely than others and this can lead to a "best guess" strategy. The ending *-le* is far more common than the endings *-el, -il,* or *-al,* and *-er* is much more common than *-or* or *-ar.* Students will also learn that comparative adjectives (*bigger, better*) are always spelled with *-er.* Students will:

* Identify the unaccented syllable and learn the appropriate spelling patterns
* Know when to change the *y* to *i* before *-ed* and *-s*
* Spell the words in these sorts correctly

Targeted Learners

These sorts are designed for students in the middle syllable and affixes stage who are making errors such as BOTTEL for *bottle,* FAVER for *favor,* and RIPIN for *ripen.* Spell Check 5 on page 77 can be used as a pretest to more thoroughly assess the features covered in these sorts. Students who score 90% or better can move on to other sorts.

Teaching Tips

The standard weekly routines described on pages 6–7 are important for the extra practice and extensions they offer. Word hunts in daily reading materials will turn up additional words for most of these sorts and will help students develop a sense of the frequency of certain final unaccented syllable spellings. You may want to create class lists of all the words students find for each category to enhance these discoveries.

Create games and activities such as those in Chapters 6 and 7 of *WTW*. Apple and Bushel in Chapter 7 will work well for words that end in *-el* and *-le* and can be adapted for other unaccented syllables. Dinosaur Take-a-Card (for *-el, -le, -il,* and *-al*) and Feed the Alligator (for *-an, -in, -on,* and *-ain*) can be downloaded ready to use from the CD-ROM, and these games can also be adapted for other endings.

Some of the words in these sorts may not be well known, so we urge you to discuss their meanings before introducing the sort. You may want students to look up the meanings of some words to add to the discussion.

SORT 29   UNACCENTED FINAL SYLLABLE (LE)

Demonstrate

(See page 78.) Prepare a set of words to use for teacher-directed modeling. Write up the words *super, butter,* and *basket* and remind students of the syllable juncture patterns they assigned to these words: VCV and VCCV (with and without doublets). Underline the corresponding letters in the words, as in the *u, p,* and *e* of the VCV pattern in *super.* Tell your students that they will be reviewing juncture patterns in the words for this week. Hand out or show an overhead of all the words and ask students what they notice (e.g., all have two syllables, all end with *-le*). Go over any words students might not know. Put up the headers and key words (*title, little,* and *simple*) and point out the syllable juncture pattern that precedes the ending of *-le.* Explain to students that *-le* is always connected to a consonant and the syllable juncture patterns are modified to reflect this. For example, VCV is now represented as VCle. Sort the rest of the words with the students' help.

Talk about how the words in each column are alike. Point out how the VCle pattern in *title* is divided after the vowel to make the open syllable (*ti-tle*) with a long-vowel sound, whereas the VCCle pattern in *little* and *simple* is divided between the consonants, resulting in closed syllables (*lit-tle* and *sim-ple*) with short vowels. Ask your students: *Which words will have open syllables with long-vowel sounds in the first syllable? Which words will have closed syllables with short-vowel sounds in the first syllable?*

Review accent or syllable stress by asking students what they notice when they read the columns of words. In these words the stress always falls on the first syllable, making the second and last syllables *unaccented.* Students might be directed to the dictionary to look up several words and see how the final syllable is represented in the pronunciation guide for the word. Explain that the upside-down e (ə) is called a *schwa* sound. (Note: Dictionaries differ. Check in advance to see how these sounds are represented.)

VCle		VCCle doublet		VCCle	
title	rifle	**little***	apple	**simple**	sample
cradle	bridle	middle	paddle	tremble	jungle
able	bugle	settle	giggle	single	handle
table	cable	bottle	battle	muscle	candle

*High-frequency word

Sort, Check, and Reflect

After modeling the sort, have students cut apart and shuffle their cards and sort them using the same headers and key words. After the students sort, have them check their own sorts by looking for the pattern in each column. If students do not notice a mistake, guide them to it by saying: *One of these doesn't fit. See if you can find it.* Encourage reflections by asking the students how the words in each column are alike and how they are different from the other words.

Extend

Word hunts will turn up lots of words that end in *-le,* including some that will have a different vowel pattern associated with a familiar syllable juncture pattern (such as *double*), which can go in an oddball category. See the list of standard weekly routines for follow-up activities to the basic sorting lesson.

Additional Words.   *fable, idle, noble, maple, eagle, cycle, bible, rattle, puddle, wriggle, pebble, scribble, juggle, muffle, struggle, bubble, puzzle, fiddle, scramble, sprinkle, twinkle, crackle, mumble, bundle, tangle, tickle*

SORT 30   UNACCENTED FINAL SYLLABLE
(*LE, EL, IL, AL*)

Demonstrate, Sort, Check, and Reflect

(See page 79.) You may want to introduce this with a short spelling test. Ask students to spell *cattle, model, pencil,* and *final.* Talk about what makes the words hard to spell (they all have the same /əl/ sound in the final unaccented syllable). If you start with a student-directed sort, cut off the headers before making copies. Hand out the words and go over any that students might not know. Discuss the multiple meanings of *novel.* Ask the students what they notice about all the words and elicit ideas about how they might sort them. Students might suggest sorting by syllable juncture patterns as they did in the previous sort, or they might suggest sorting by the spelling in the final syllable as shown in the sort below. Read the columns of words to discover where the accent falls in the words. You may want to focus on the words *angle* and *angel* and speculate about why they are spelled as they are (the *g* in *angel* is "softened" by the following *e* but remains hard before the *l* in *angle*).

-le	-el	-il	-al	oddball
cattle	**model**	**until***	**final**	fragile
saddle	level	April	total	special
couple	angel	fossil	metal	
angle	novel	evil	signal	
	cancel	pencil	local	
	vowel		journal	
	travel			

*Among the top 300 high-frequency words

Extend

A word hunt will be useful with this sort. Although the *-le* column is quite short here, it is by far the most common spelling and will turn up in word hunts with the greatest frequency. Words spelled with *-el* are not too rare, but students will find it challenging to find more words for the *-il* and *-al* categories. At some point, compile a list of all the words students have found, including the words from last week, and talk about the relative frequencies of each. Ask students to form a best guess strategy if they hear the sound in a word that they are not sure how to spell. How would they spell the name *Mable*? Or the word *frindle*? (*Frindle* is the name of a book by Andrew Clements in which a boy decides to invent a new word and, of course, has to invent a spelling for it also.) Apple and Bushel, described in Chapter 7 of *WTW,* is designed to differentiate between *-el* and *-le* endings and can be adapted to include *-il* and *-al* as well. Dinosaur Take-a-Card, available on the CD-ROM, reviews all four.

Additional Words.   *dimple, tingle, freckle, huddle, kennel, label, towel, shovel, channel, camel, gravel, peril, tonsil, pupil, civil, council, scandal, neutral, crystal, global, medal, oval, tidal, plural, fertile, hostile*

SORT 31   UNACCENTED FINAL SYLLABLE (ER, AR, OR)

Demonstrate, Sort, Check, and Reflect

(See page 80.) You might begin this sort with a short spelling test in which you ask students to spell three words: *cover, doctor,* and *collar.* As in previous sorts, compare their spellings as a way to highlight the problem spellers face when they can hear the same sound in the final unaccented syllable but are not sure how to spell it. Show students the words for this week and talk about the meaning of any that may be unfamiliar. Read them aloud to enforce the idea that the final sound is exactly the same in all the words but has several spellings. Ask them to hypothesize about which one is most common. Proceed with a teacher-directed or student-centered sort that will look something like the sort below. Review the idea of accent or stress by reading the columns of words to find that the final syllable in these words (e.g., words ending in /ər/) is unaccented. Again, have students use the dictionary to check how the unaccented syllable is represented in the pronunciation guide.

-er		-or		-ar
other*	under*	**color***	motor	**collar**
mother*	father	doctor	rumor	dollar
weather	flower	favor	tractor	solar
cover	spider	flavor	harbor	sugar
silver	rather	mirror		grammar

*Among the top 300 high-frequency words

Extend

As described for Sort 30, use a word hunt to answer the question of frequency and compile a master list of all the words students can find. You can also challenge students to sort the words they find by parts of speech. They will find many adjectives and nouns that will anticipate the sort for next week.

Additional Words.   stranger, brother, bother, center, proper, roller, rubber, crater, printer, fiber, liter, litter, lumber, manner, horror, razor, splendor, terror, tremor, vapor, tumor, error, cedar, cheddar, lunar, molar, polar, nectar, liar

SORT 32   AGENTS AND COMPARATIVES

Demonstrate, Sort, Check, and Reflect

(See page 81.) You might begin the study of agents (i.e., people who do things) and comparatives by looking at the master word hunt list from Sort 31. Ask students to find words that name people who do things (agents). Ask them if there is another category of words they can find. Prompt them by asking how words like *bigger* and *older* (select comparative words from your list) are alike. Explain that these words can be called *comparative adjectives.* Begin this two-step sort by using the headers and sorting all the words into two categories. Then pull out the key words to head up subcategories and sort the words further by the spelling of the final unaccented syllable.

People Who Do Things			Words Used to Compare
dancer	**actor**	**beggar**	**bigger**
dreamer	sailor	burglar	sooner
driver	traitor		longer
farmer	tutor		smaller
jogger			fresher
writer			younger
shopper			older
swimmer			smoother
voter			brighter

Extend

Write up the word *beg, begging, begged,* and *beggar.* Ask students what they notice about the spelling and review with them the rules they learned about adding *-ed* and *-ing* to words with VC at the end. Explain that similar rules ("double, *e*-drop, and nothing") apply when adding these endings to a word because the ending starts with a vowel. Repeat with *drive, driving,* and *driver.* Ask the students to sort the words for this week (that have base words) according to the rule that applies to the base word, as shown below. Have them add this sort to their word study notebook. On the weekly assessment check for transfer by asking students to spell *rubber, diver,* and *catcher.*

double	e-drop	nothing	
beggar	driver	dreamer	older
jogger	writer	farmer	smoother
swimmer	dancer	sailor	brighter
bigger	voter	sooner	longer
shopper		smaller	fresher
		younger	actor

Note: *Traitor, tutor,* and *burglar* do not have base words.

Additional Words.   *speaker, skater, racer, tailor, donor, scholar, vicar, braver, cheaper, weaker, stronger, quicker, shower, lighter, darker, tamer, wilder, hotter, cooler*

Because comparatives include a lot of antonyms you might challenge students to match pairs such as *older–younger, bigger–smaller* and to come up with antonyms for *smoother, brighter,* and *sooner.* More pairs can be found among the additional words above.

SORT 33   UNACCENTED FINAL SYLLABLES (/CHUR/ZHUR/YUR/)

Demonstrate, Sort, Check, and Reflect

(See page 82.) The unaccented final syllables in these words have two spellings (*-er* and *-ure*) and several sounds (/chur/, /zhur/, and /yur/) that are similar but subtly different. Although we ask students to sort by the sounds, do not be overly concerned if there is disagreement and inconsistency. The point is not as much to sort the words correctly by sound, as it is to see that the words are spelled with the same pattern (*-ure*) despite these slight differences. Because this is a more challenging sort, model it in a teacher-directed sort. Put up the headers and a key word for each. Explain that the slash marks indicate a sound that goes with the spelling pattern above and pronounce them for the students. Say each key word and stress the sound in the final syllable. Sort the rest of the words, taking the time to say each word, and have the students repeat it and then compare it to the key words or headers before sorting. *Senior* and *danger* are odd-balls that have similar sounds but different spellings.

-cher = /chur/	*-ture* = /chur/	*-sure* = /zhur/	*-ure* = /yur/	oddball
catcher	**picture**	**measure**	**figure**	senior
rancher	nature	pressure**	failure	danger
teacher	capture	pleasure		
pitcher	future	leisure		
	mixture	treasure		
	creature			
	pasture			
	posture			
	torture			
	culture			
	injure			

**Might be closer to /shur/ than /zhur/ to some ears

Additional Words.   *stretcher, marcher, fracture, juncture, texture, lecture, puncture, secure, endure, obscure, conjure*

Extend

The game You're Up in Chapter 7 of *WTW* is designed to reinforce the spelling of these words.

SORT 34   UNACCENTED FINAL SYLLABLES (*EN, ON, AIN, IN*)

Demonstrate, Sort, Check, and Reflect

(See page 83.) Students should be able to do this as an open sort using the spelling patterns in the final syllable. Use word hunts to determine the best guess strategy based on frequency.

-en	*-on*	*-ain*	*-in*	oddball
broken	**dragon**	**mountain**	**cousin**	mission
eleven	cotton	captain	cabin	
hidden	gallon	bargain	napkin	
heaven	ribbon	fountain	penguin	
chosen	prison	curtain	muffin	
stolen	bacon			
mitten				

Additional Words.   *golden, rotten, spoken, swollen, button, apron, weapon, carton, villain, chieftain, basin, satin, margin, robin*

   Words ending in *-an* might be contrasted also: *woman, organ, orphan, slogan, urban,* and *human.*

Extend

See Feed the Alligator on the CD-ROM.

SORT 35 UNACCENTED FINAL SYLLABLES (*ET, IT, ATE*)

(See page 84.) In these sorts the final unaccented syllable sound is spelled three ways. You may want to ask your students to look up the origin of the oddballs. Both are derived from French where the final *t* is often silent as in *valet, beret, fillet, sachet,* and *chalet.*

-et	-it	-ate	oddball
jacket	**edit**	**climate**	ballet
secret	unit	private	buffet
target	credit	pirate	
racket	limit	senate	
quiet	habit		
comet	orbit		
rocket	summit		
closet	bandit		
magnet	merit		

Additional Words. *wicket, bonnet, bullet, faucet, digit, hermit*

SORT 36 FINAL -Y, -EY, AND -IE

(See page 85.) Final *-y* usually has the sound of long *-e* when it is the unaccented syllable in a two-syllable word (*candy, very*). It has the long *-i* sound in one-syllable words such as *fly, sky, shy,* etc., and words in which the final syllable is accented as in *July* and *deny.* Sort these words in a manner similar to that described in Sort 35. Students should be successful sorting these in an open sort but you may need to have them sort again by the sound of the final *-y.*

-ey	-ie	-y = e	-y = i
money*	**cookie**	**very***	**July**
monkey	movie	candy	deny
journey	brownie	dizzy	reply
valley	goalie	twenty	
turkey	eerie	cherry	
donkey	pinkie	body	
volley		story	
		berry	

*Among the top 300 high-frequency words

Additional Words. *alley, chimney, honey, jockey, jersey, pulley, hockey, genie, sweetie, zombie, bootie, rookie, prairie, family, baby, duty, forty, beauty, crazy, gravy, army, fifty, empty, tidy, ruby, envy, bury, treaty, bossy, easy, lady, apply, defy, supply*

SORT 37   Y + INFLECTED ENDINGS

Demonstrate, Sort, Check, and Reflect

(See page 86.) Students were introduced to changing the *-y* before inflected endings in Sort 9 but here it is studied further in two-syllable words. Students should see that the *-y* is changed to *i* after a consonant (as in *copy* to *copied*) but not after a vowel (as in *obey* to *obeyed*). Start by having students underline the base in the words that end in *-ing* under the heading *+ ing*. Talk about how the base words are alike and different. Then add words with the same base under each of the other headings as shown below. Ask students for observations: *What do you notice?* They should see that the *y* does not change to an *i* before *ing*. (Show them how this would look: *repling* or *replying*.) It changes to *i* before *-s* and *-ed* when the base word ends in a consonant + *y*.

	+ ing	*+ ed*	*+ s*
vowel + *y*	*obey*ing	obeyed	obeys
	*enjoy*ing	enjoyed	enjoys
	*decay*ing	decayed	decays
consonant + *y*	*reply*ing	replied	replies
	*study*ing	studied	studies
	*copy*ing	copied	copies
	*carry*ing	carried	carries
	*hurry*ing	hurried	hurries

Extend

To practice transfer of the rules to other words, give students these nouns from the last sort to change to plurals: *monkey, body, cherry, valley, berry, donkey,* and *turkey.* Give them these verbs and ask them to add *-ing, -ed,* and *-s* to change the tense: *journey, deny, reply.* You can also add these: *envy, survey, worry, bury,* and *supply.*

SORT 38   UNACCENTED INITIAL SYLLABLES (*A-, DE-, BE-*)

(See page 87.) In these words the first syllable is unaccented and has the schwa sound (ə-*gain,* də-*bate,* bə-*yond*). Some of these words (*among, awhile, because*) appeared in a within word pattern sort but are revisited here. Many rank as "spelling demons" that students struggle to spell across the grades. As in final unaccented syllables, students should be led to see that sound cannot always be trusted as a guide to spelling the unaccented syllable in these words. Nevertheless, the words fall into categories that share similar spelling patterns. Expect some lively debate about the exact pronunciation of some of these words. We sometimes stress a different syllable when we say a word in isolation or when we are thinking about the spelling. For example, we might say <u>be</u>*yond* with a long *-e* vowel sound at times, but when we use it in a sentence we probably say /bə-yond/. Stressing normally unaccented syllables is actually a good spelling strategy that works well with words like these and you might suggest that to your students. Although we may disagree about the exact sound and syllable stress, the spelling patterns can clearly be sorted as shown below. The oddballs include a few words that have the schwa sound in the first syllable but a different spelling pattern.

You might begin with a sound sort and then look for words that do not fit the patterns to find the oddballs.

a-	de-	be-	oddball
away*	**debate**	**because***	divide
another*	degree	believe	direct
awhile	depend	between	upon
along*	desire	beneath	
among	develop	beyond	
against	defend	begun	
afraid			
aloud			
agreed			

*Among the top 300 high-frequency words

Additional Words.   *around, again, ago, alike, alive, asleep, ahead, another, begin, below, beside, beware, belong, beyond, before, defeat, describe, despair* (some of these have appeared in earlier sorts)

SPELL CHECK 5   ASSESSMENT FOR UNACCENTED SYLLABLES

Retention Test

The words below have been selected from previous lessons. Call them aloud for students to spell on a sheet of notebook paper. You can also ask students to rewrite them into categories and explain why they grouped them together.

1. carried	**2.** capture	**3.** model	**4.** gallon
5. afraid	**6.** favor	**7.** measure	**8.** title
9. eleven	**10.** April	**11.** signal	**12.** dollar
13. degree	**14.** younger	**15.** copying	**16.** middle
17. napkin	**18.** because	**19.** tutor	**20.** weather

SORT 29   Unaccented Final Syllable (*le*)

VCle	VCCle doublet	VCCle
title	**little**	**simple**
middle	able	tremble
cable	single	settle
bottle	table	muscle
cradle	apple	paddle
giggle	jungle	bridle
bugle	battle	handle
candle	sample	rifle

SORT 30   Unaccented Final Syllable (*le, el, il, al*)

-le	*-el*	*-al*	*-il*
cattle	model		final
until	level		April
total	saddle		angel
novel	fossil		metal
couple	cancel		fragile
travel	special		vowel
signal	journal		angle
evil	pencil		local

SORT 31   Unaccented Final Syllable (*er, ar, or*)

-er	*-or*	*-ar*
other	**color**	**collar**
doctor	spider	sugar
rather	dollar	favor
solar	cover	silver
weather	flavor	mother
flower	father	mirror
under	rumor	motor
tractor	grammar	harbor

SORT 32   Agents and Comparatives

People who do things	Words used to compare	
dancer	**bigger**	**actor**
beggar	dreamer	sooner
longer	smaller	driver
farmer	burglar	traitor
fresher	jogger	younger
writer	older	sailor
smoother	swimmer	brighter
tutor	shopper	voter

SORT 33   Unaccented Final Syllables (/chur/zhur/yur/)

-cher = /chur/	*-ture* = /chur/	*-sure* = /zhur/	*-ure* = /yur/
catcher		**picture**	**measure**
figure	danger		failure
pressure	rancher		capture
future	nature		treasure
teacher	mixture		senior
pleasure	creature		culture
pasture	leisure		pitcher
injure	torture		posture

SORT 34   Unaccented Final Syllables (*en*, *on*, *ain*, *in*)

-en	*-on*	*-ain*	*-in*
broken	**dragon**	**mountain**	
cousin	eleven	cotton	
gallon	captain	hidden	
heaven	cabin	ribbon	
bargain	chosen	napkin	
mission	muffin	fountain	
stolen	bacon	mitten	
prison	curtain	penguin	

SORT 35   Unaccented Final Syllables (*et, it, ate*)

-et	*-it*	*-ate*	*oddball*
jacket	**edit**	**climate**	
secret	private	unit	
ballet	target	credit	
pirate	racket	limit	
senate	buffet	quiet	
habit	comet	rocket	
summit	closet	bandit	
orbit	magnet	merit	

SORT 36   Final -y, -ey, and -ie

-ey	-ie	-y = e	-y = i
money	**cookie**	**very**	
July	monkey	movie	
candy	deny	journey	
brownie	dizzy	reply	
valley	goalie	twenty	
turkey	eerie	cherry	
donkey	story	body	
volley	pinkie	berry	

SORT 37   y + Inflected Endings

+ ing	+ ed	+ s
obeying	enjoying	replying
hurrying	obeyed	enjoyed
obeys	hurried	decaying
hurries	decayed	enjoys
decays	carried	copying
replies	studying	carrying
carries	studies	copied
studied	copies	replied

SORT 38   Unaccented Initial Syllables (*a-*, *de-*, *be-*)

a-	*de-*	*be-*	*oddball*
away	**debate**		**because**
degree	another		believe
divide	depend		awhile
along	between		desire
develop	among		upon
against	beneath		afraid
beyond	aloud		defend
agreed	begun		direct

Unit VI   Exploring Consonants

NOTES FOR THE TEACHER

Background and Objectives

Consonants continue to be explored at all levels of spelling. Hard and soft *g* and *c* were introduced in the within word pattern stage but are revisited here at the beginning and end of longer words. Whether the sound of *g* or *c* is hard or soft depends on the vowel that follows it, and this can account for some interesting spellings. Sort 39 looks at initial hard and soft *g* and *c*. This sort lays the foundation for Sorts 40 and 41, where hard and soft generalizations apply to words that end in *-ge* and *-ce*, and explains why there is a place holder (the letter *u*) between *g* and *i* in the word *guide* and between *g* and *e* in the word *tongue*. Without the *u*, the sound of *g* would become soft (/jide/ or /tonj/).

The spelling of the /k/ sound in English is not as simple as most consonant sounds in words of more than one syllable. Although students learned the final *ck* in relation to short vowels in the within word pattern stage, *ck* is revisited here in the middle of two-syllable words. Other /k/ spellings, such as *ic*, *x*, and *que*, are also explored in Sorts 42 and 43.

Words with silent letters at the beginning (*honest*, *knuckle*) and in the middle of words (*listen*, *thought*) are examined in Sort 44. *Ph* consistently spells the sound of /f/, usually in words that derive from Greek. *Gh* is often silent but can also represent the sound of /f/ at the end of some words. Some more advanced vocabulary that foreshadows the study of Greek combining forms in derivational relations will be covered in Sort 45. Students will:

- Understand the role of silent *-e* after *g* and *c*
- Spell the words in these sorts correctly

Targeted Learners

These sorts are designed for students in the middle to late syllable and affixes stage. Spell Check 6 on page 94 can be used as a pretest. Students who spell 90% or more of the words can move on to other features.

Teaching Tips

The standard weekly routines (pages 6–7) will work well with these sorts. The meaning of some words in these sorts may not be familiar, so you should discuss these before introducing the sort. Students should be encouraged to look up some meanings of words to add to the discussion. A few words might also be assigned to look up for a word study notebook activity.

SORT 39   INITIAL HARD AND SOFT *G* AND *C*

Demonstrate

(See page 95.) This sort has several steps, so allow extra time, or do it over several days. Read over the words and talk about any that might be unfamiliar. Begin by sorting the words into two columns by the beginning letter (*g* or *c*). Then read all the words in the *c* column and ask students what they notice about the sound spelled with *c* at the beginning (sometimes it sounds like /k/ and sometimes like /s/). Explain that these sounds are called **hard** *c* and **soft** *c* and introduce the headers. Sort by hard and soft *g* and *c*. The sort will look something like the following:

Sort by Initial Sounds

Soft *c*	Soft *g*	Hard *c*	Hard *g*
cement	**gentle**	**correct**	**gather**
circle	gymnast	common	gossip
central	giraffe	contest	golden
century	genius	college	garage
cyclist	general	custom	gutter
cider	gingerbread	collect	
cereal			

Next, combine all the soft *g* and soft *c* words. Ask students if they notice anything about the vowel in these words. Repeat this with the hard *c* and hard *g* words. Suggest that they try sorting the words by the second letter in each word. The final sort will reveal that the hard and soft sounds are related to the vowel that follows. Underline the vowel that follows the *c* or *g* as a key word for each column. This sort will look something like the following:

Sort by Vowel that Follows the Initial Letter

Soft *g* and Soft *c*			Hard *g* and Hard *c*		
c<u>e</u>ment	c<u>i</u>rcle	c<u>y</u>clist	g<u>a</u>ther	c<u>o</u>rrect	c<u>u</u>stom
central	cider	gymnast	garage	common	gutter
century	giraffe			contest	
cereal				college	
gentle				collect	
genius				gossip	
general				golden	
gingerbread					

Sort, Check, and Reflect

After modeling the sort, have students cut apart and sort their own words into both sorts. You might have them underline the vowel to create headers for the second sort as shown above and to check after sorting. Encourage reflections by asking the students how the words in each column are alike and how they are different from the other words. Help students formulate a generalization that goes something like this: *C* and *g* are usually soft when followed by *e, i,* or *y* and hard when followed by *a, o,* or *u.*

Additional Words.   *gallon, gamble, gully, gorilla, gopher, gather, gobble, genie, gerbil, ginger, gypsy, gyrate, gently, gender, cactus, candle, cavern, comma, cozy, cocoa, coffee, cuddle, concern, concert, city, cedar, celery, census, cellar, center, certain, ceiling, cynic, cycle, cymbal, cyclone* (some of these have appeared in earlier sorts)

Extend

Students should repeat these sorts several times and record them in their word study notebook. See the list of standard weekly routines for follow-up activities to the basic sorting lesson. Word hunts may not turn up many more two-syllable words with the soft *g* and *c*, but accept one-syllable words, such as *camp* and *goat*, and expect some oddballs, such as *girl* and *gift*. To anticipate the next sort, point out the final sound and spelling in college and garage. Ask students to speculate about why their is a final *e* in those words.

SORT 40   S AND SOFT C AND G IN THE FINAL SYLLABLE

Demonstrate, Sort, Check, and Reflect

(See page 96.) Go over the words to read and discuss their meanings. Remind students that in the previous sort they looked at the sounds of hard and soft *g* at the beginnings of words. Explain that now they will examine soft *g* (/j/) and *c* (/s/) at the ends of words. Ask them what they notice about the words in this sort. Talk about possible headers and then sort the words, starting with the key words. Remind students that letters inside slanted lines, /j/ for example, represent a sound. Talk about how words in each column are alike by sound and the spelling pattern used to spell the sound. *Surgeon* might be an oddball or go under the *-ge-* pattern. Talk about how *surgeon* would have to be pronounced if the *e* were dropped: /surgon/. Do the same thing with words under *-ce*. If the *e* were dropped in the word *notice* we would probably want to say /notick/. Repeat with other words to help students reflect on why these words have an *-e* after the *c* or *g*. Help students form a generalization such as the following: At the end of words the final sound of /s/ can be spelled *-ce* or *-ss* and the soft sound of *g* is often followed by the letter *e*.

ce = /s/	ss = /s/	-ge- = /j/	age = /ij/
notice	**recess**	**budget**	**bandage**
police	princess	midget	garbage
sentence	actress	gadget	manage
distance	address	surgeon**	luggage
office	compass		package
science			village
practice			message
			courage

**Surgeon* may be sorted as an oddball.

Additional Words.   *absence, announce, lettuce, fragrance, possess, success, express, congress, challenge, arrange, submerge, baggage, beverage, carriage, cottage, damage, image, marriage, passage, postage, savage, storage, sausage, voyage, wreckage*

Extend

Review plurals by asking students to add *-s* or *-es* to these words from the sort: *princess, actress, address*. Review the final sound in *college, voyage,* and *garage* from earlier sorts.

SORT 41   MORE WORDS WITH *G*

Demonstrate, Sort, Check, and Reflect

(See page 97.) Introduce this sort in a manner similar to Sort 40. In these words the sound of *g* is always hard because it is followed by a placeholder, the silent letter *u*, to separate it from a vowel that would otherwise make it soft. *Guard* is somewhat of an oddball because it really does not need the *u* to keep the *g* hard before the letter *a*. The other oddballs offer a chance to talk about the sound of *g* in each one. In *gauge* there is both a hard and a soft *g*, but no apparent reason for the *u*. In *language* the final *-age* is similar to words from the previous sort, but the *u* takes on a /w/ sound as it does in *penguin* from Sort 34. In *argue*, the *u* represents the long sound as well as keeping the *g* hard. Help students reflect on these words and form a generalization such as the following: Silent *u* is sometimes used to keep the *g* hard before *e* and *i*.

gu-	-gue	-g		oddball
guess	**tongue**	**ladybug**	dialog**	gauge
guard	vague	zigzag		language
guitar	league	shrug		argue
guide	fatigue	iceberg		
guilty	plague	strong		
guest	intrigue	catalog**		

***Catalogue* and *dialogue* are alternative spellings for these words.

Extend

Word hunts may not be very productive with these spellings. Have students look up *catalog* and *dialog* in the dictionary to see if there are alternative spellings for these words.

Additional Words.   *morgue, rogue, vogue, prologue, mustang. Gu* serves as the same blend (/gw/) in words of Spanish origin such as *guacamole, iguana, saguaro, guava,* and *guano* as it does in *language, penguin, anguish,* and *languish.* ELLs might supply more Spanish words with the *gu* spelling.

SORT 42   THE SOUND OF *K* SPELLED *CK*, *IC*, AND *X*

Demonstrate, Sort, Check, and Reflect

(See page 98.) Introduce this sort in a manner similar to the other sorts in this unit, noting how the /k/ sound (or /ks/ in the case of *x*) in the middle and end of these words is spelled with *ck, ic,* and *x*. *Stomach* is an oddball because it ends in a sound like /ick/ but is spelled in an unusual way. A word hunt will turn up many one-syllable words that end in *k* and may help students conclude that while one-syllable words that end in the /k/ sound are always spelled with *-k* (*leak*) or *-ck* (*lack*), most two-syllable words end in *-ic* except for compound words like *homesick.*

-ck	-ck-	-ic	-x	oddball
shock	**chicken**	**magic**	**relax**	stomach
quick	pocket	attic	index	
hammock	nickel	traffic	perplex	
attack	pickle	topic	complex	
	buckle	picnic		
	ticket	metric		
		frantic		
		fabric		
		plastic		

Additional Words. *paddock, ransack, gimmick, limerick, chuckle, cricket, electric, freckle, clinic, panic, Arctic, music, mimic, scenic, public, skeptic, comic, prefix, annex, vortex, vertex, Xerox, reflex, phoenix* (some of these words may have appeared in earlier sorts)

Extend

The game Double Crazy Eights, described in Chapter 7 of *WTW*, is designed to review the *k* and *ck* spellings and also review the rules of adding inflected endings to such words. When adding *-ing* or *-ed* to *picnic*, a final *k* must be added to keep the *c* from being "softened."

SORT 43   SPELLINGS WITH QU

(See page 99.) Introduce this sort by asking how the words are all alike and talk about possible ways to sort them. The letters *q* and *u* together spell the /kw/ blend that can come in the first or second syllable of these words. *Qu* occasionally spells just the sound of /k/, as it does in the last column of words. Point out that *racquet* has a homophone spelled *racket* and talk about what both words mean.

1st syllable		2nd syllable		qu = /k/
question	quiver	**equal**	banquet	**antique**
quality	quizzes	frequent	inquire	racquet
squirrel	queasy	tranquil	liquid	mosquito
squirm	squeaky	request	require	conquer
quaint		sequel	sequence	technique

Additional Words. *quarrel, quarter, quotient, equip, quotation, squabble, squiggle, qualify, equation, acquaint, acquire, vanquish, critique, mosque, boutique, bouquet, clique, croquet* (some of these may have appeared in earlier sorts)

SORT 44   WORDS WITH SILENT CONSONANTS

Demonstrate, Sort, Check, and Reflect

(See page 100.) Go over these words to talk about the meaning of any that are unfamiliar. Ask students to figure out how these words are all alike (each one has a silent consonant). Introduce the headers and key words or let students establish the categories. The word *wrestle* has two silent letters and can go in two categories. Students should be challenged to find more words with silent consonants, and their search may turn up many familiar one-syllable words like *write*, *light*, and *knife*. Note that the second syllable in rhythm has no vowel, a rare instance in English where every syllable usually has a vowel.

Silent *t*	Silent *g*	Silent *w*	Silent *k*	Silent *h*	Silent *gh*
castle	**design**	**wrinkle**	**knuckle**	**honest**	**through**
whistle	resign	wreckage	knowledge	honor	thought
fasten	assign	(wrestle)		rhyme	brought
listen		answer		rhythm	bought
often					though*
soften					
(wrestle)					

Additional Words.   *thistle, hustle, glisten, bristle, moisten, bustle, align, gnaw, phlegm, campaign, foreign, wreath, wrong, knead, knight, knock, rhinoceros, shepherd, rhombus*

SORT 45   *GH* AND *PH*

(See page 101.) Discuss the meaning of any words that might be unfamiliar to students such as *phantom*. Introduce this sort in a manner similar to the other sorts in this unit, noting how *ph* and *gh* represent /f/ and how *gh* is often silent in the middle of words. Remind students of the words from last week that had silent *gh* (*through, thought*, etc.). More of these spelling demons are revisited this week. Words hunts may not turn up many more words for these spelling features.

ph-	*-ph-*	*gh* = /f/	silent *gh*
phrase	**alphabet**	**enough**	**daughter**
physics	dolphin	cough	naughty
phantom	elephant	tough	taught
phone	nephew	rough	caught
	orphan	laughter	fought
	trophy		
	triumph		
	paragraph		

Additional Words.   *spherical, prophet, photograph, photocopy, physical, phonics, telephone, homophone, autograph*

SPELL CHECK 6   ASSESSMENT FOR CONSONANTS

Retention Test

The words below have been selected from previous lessons. Call them aloud for students to spell on a sheet of notebook paper. You can then ask your students to rewrite them into categories and explain why they grouped them together.

1. central	**2.** gossip	**3.** attack	**4.** sentence
5. plastic	**6.** equal	**7.** listen	**8.** contest
9. genius	**10.** ticket	**11.** village	**12.** guilty
13. index	**14.** answer	**15.** liquid	**16.** thought
17. trophy	**18.** address	**19.** vague	**20.** enough

SORT 39   Initial Hard and Soft *g* and *c*

Soft *c*	Hard *c*	Soft *g*	Hard *g*
cement		gentle	correct
gather	circle		common
gossip	gutter		golden
central	contest		college
giraffe	garage		century
custom	cereal		genius
cider	general		collect
gingerbread	gymnast		cyclist

SORT 40   *s* and Soft *c* and *g* in the Final Syllable

ce = /s/	*ss* = /s/	*ge* = /j/	*age* = /ij/
notice	**recess**		**budget**
bandage	police		princess
midget	garbage		sentence
science	actress		manage
luggage	office		gadget
address	message		practice
package	compass		village
distance	surgeon		courage

SORT 41   More Words with *g*

gu-	*-gue*	*-g*	*oddball*
guess	**tongue**	**ladybug**	
gauge	zigzag	vague	
league	guard	shrug	
fatigue	iceberg	catalog	
guitar	language	guide	
guilty	plague	intrigue	
argue	guest	strong	
dialog			

SORT 42   The Sound of *k* Spelled *ck, ic,* and *x*

-ck	**-ck-**	**-ic**	**-x**
shock		**chicken**	**magic**
relax		quick	pocket
attic		nickel	traffic
complex		topic	stomach
pickle		picnic	attack
metric		buckle	index
fabric		frantic	ticket
hammock		plastic	perplex

SORT 43   Spellings with *qu*

1st syllable	2nd syllable	*qu* = /k/
question	**equal**	**antique**
frequent	quality	tranquil
squirrel	liquid	racquet
require	squirm	inquire
quaint	technique	sequence
sequel	quiver	conquer
quizzes	banquet	request
squeaky	mosquito	queasy

SORT 44   Words with Silent Consonants

silent t	silent g	silent w	silent k	silent h	silent gh
castle		design		wrinkle	
honest		through		knuckle	
bought		whistle		honor	
fasten		resign		wrestle	
rhyme		listen		thought	
often		brought		knowledge	
wreckage		soften		rhythm	
assign		though		answer	

SORT 45   *gh* and *ph*

ph-	-ph-	gh = /f/	silent *gh*
phrase	**alphabet**	**enough**	
daughter	physics	dolphin	
elephant	cough	nephew	
tough	phantom	naughty	
orphan	laughter	trophy	
rough	triumph	taught	
caught	phone	fought	
paragraph			

Unit VII   Affixes

NOTES FOR THE TEACHER

Background and Objectives

The term "affixes" includes prefixes and suffixes and both will be introduced as meaning units (or morphemes) in these seven sorts. Unlike the inflected suffixes studied earlier, the affixes in these sorts change the meaning of the word (*lock* becomes the opposite *unlock*) or the part of speech (the verb *love* becomes the adjective *lovely* or *loveable*). The suffix *-er*, which can indicate agents and comparatives, has already been introduced although it was not identified as a suffix at the time. It will be revisited in Sort 51 where it is added to words that end in *-y*.

In these sorts much more attention will be paid to the meaning of the words **after** they are sorted rather than before, so we suggest you skip the usual practice of reading and discussing the meanings of unfamiliar words as the first step. These sorts foreshadow the derivational relations stage where meaning and the learning of new vocabulary take on greater importance in word study activities. The words in these sorts, however, are likely to be words that are known to most students (especially the base words) and the focus is upon learning about base words and affixes as meaning units that can be combined in many different ways. Often the spelling of these words is not especially challenging (*refill, unfair,* or even *carelessness*), being made up of base words that are very familiar and affixes that are spelled regularly. However, working with the sorts helps students see words and think of words as being made up of "chunks" or word parts that share meanings and spelling patterns. Students will:

- Identify and spell prefixes and suffixes
- Articulate how the addition of affixes changes the meaning or use of the word
- Spell the words correctly in these sorts

Targeted Learners

We have placed these sorts here in the later part of the syllables and affixes stage as a transition into the next stage of derivational relations. However, these sorts can be used earlier if desired. Sometimes language arts standards stipulate the study of prefixes in second or third grade. As long as students can read and understand the base words (such as *mature* in *premature*) they can benefit from these sorts. Words that have a familiar base word have been selected in this introduction to prefixes. Spell Check 7 on page 110 can be used as a pretest to determine if students are ready to study these words. Students who score between 50% and 75% would be at an instructional level.

Teaching Tips

See pages 6–7 for the weekly routine activities. Because suffixes change the base words' part of speech [e.g., *care* (a verb) becomes *careless* or *careful* (adjectives) and *carefully* (an adverb)], this is a good time to introduce or review parts of speech as part of your general language arts program. Students can sort words by their part of speech as an extension to the other sorts.

In several of these sorts, students will be asked to recall and extend their knowledge of the rules covered earlier under inflected endings. They will find that the "double, drop, or nothing" and the "change *y* to *i*" rules will come into play when *-y*, *-ly*, *-er*, and *-est* are added to base words.

The study of prefixes in the upper grades is a good time to introduce dictionaries that have information about the origins of words. Interesting discoveries about base words and roots can be made, such as the relationship between using dental floss and indenting paragraphs (see Sort 48). We encourage you to have at least one dictionary available with derivational information in the classroom and many online dictionaries will have this information as well. One source is *The American Heritage Dictionary* at http://www.yourdictionary.com. Another is http://www.onelook.com.

Games from *WTW* that can be adapted for the features explored in this unit include Jeopardy, Card Categories, Word Study Pursuit, Word Study Uno, and others described in Chapter 6. The game of Match, described in Chapter 5, can be adapted for affixes. Prefix Spin is described in Chapter 7.

SORT 46   PREFIXES (*RE-, UN-*)

Demonstrate

(See page 111.) Prepare a set of words to use for teacher-directed modeling. Save the discussion of word meanings until after sorting. Display a transparency of the words on the overhead or hand out the sheet of words to the students. Ask them what they notice about the words and get ideas about how the words can be sorted. Students might note that the words all contain smaller words; remind them of the term **base words** that was used in the study of inflected endings. Put up the headers and key words and then sort the rest of the words. During this first sort, the oddballs *uncle* and *reptile* might be included under *re-* and *un-*. They are there to help students see that these letters do not always spell a meaningful prefix added to a meaningful base word. Praise students if they notice this on the first sort!

The discussion after the first sort might go something like this: *Look at the words under* re-. *What do you notice about the meanings of these words?* Focus on the key word *rebuild*. Ask students for the base word. Explain that a **prefix** has been added to the base word and that it changes the meaning of the word. Ask students what *rebuild* means (to build something over again as in *We had to rebuild the barn after the tornado hit*). Repeat this with the other words under *re-*, talking about the meaning of each word: *Recopy* means to copy again; *recycle* means to use something again, and so on. The word *reptile* does not mean to do something again and should be transferred to the oddballs. Then explain that a prefix has a meaning of its own and ask the students what *re-* means in all the words (it means to do something again). Repeat this with the words under *un-* to determine that the prefix means "not" in words such as *unable* or *unselfish*. *Uncle* will be moved to the oddballs because it does not have a base word. Students might be asked to write the meaning of the prefix on the headers (e.g., *re-* = again, *un-* = not).

re-		un-		oddball
rebuild	retrace	**unable**	unsteady	uncle
recopy	retake	unkind	unusual	reptile
recycle	retell	unfair	unbeaten	
refill	review	uneven	unselfish	
reuse	remodel	unequal	uncertain	
rewrite		unhappy		

Sort, Check, and Reflect

Students should repeat this sort several times and work with the words using the weekly routines. When students write these words in their word study notebooks, ask them to underline the prefix in each one and write the meaning of the prefix.

Extend

Word hunts will turn up lots of words that begin with *re-* and *un-*, including more odd-balls such as *rescue*, which look like they might have a prefix until the meaning and base word are considered (sometimes these words are called false prefixes). Word hunts will also reveal other subtle variations in meaning for the prefix *re-* and *un-* , as well as words with no clear base words. Some *re-* words suggest the meaning "back" or "against" as in *restore, retort, reimburse, refund, rebound, rebate,* and *rebel.* The prefix *un-* can also suggest "the opposite of" as in *unpack* and *unwrap.*

If you have dictionaries available that give information about the origins of words, students can look up any words that they don't know the meaning of or that they have questions about. For example, the word *rebel* does not have a familiar base word that stands alone, but a root word that comes from the Latin word *bellum.* How far you want to go with this is up to you and the level of understanding your students are ready to handle. Roots as word parts that come from Greek and Latin and do not stand alone as base words are explored thoroughly in the derivational relations stage.

Additional Words. *refinish, recall, recapture, recharge, reelect, refresh, relearn, refuel, unafraid, unbroken, unclean, unclear, uncover, unlock, unreal, unripe, unplug, untangle, untie*

SORT 47   PREFIXES (*DIS-*, *MIS-*, *PRE-*)

Demonstrate, Sort, Check, and Reflect

(See page 112.) Begin this sort by asking students how to spell the word *misspell* (a word that is often misspelled). Have them speculate about why there are two *ss* in the word, but do not offer an explanation yourself. Continue with this sort in a manner similar to Sort 46; that is, sort by the prefixes and then discuss the shared meanings of the words in each column. Help students discover that *dis-* means "not" or "the opposite of," *mis-* means to do something "wrongly," and *pre-* means "before" by talking about the words in each category. Students probably know the meaning of *precious* and should be able to see that there is no base word whose meaning is changed by the prefix as there is in the other words. After discussing the meaning of the prefixes and how the prefixes change the meaning of the base word, revisit the word *misspell.* Help the students see that one *s* is part of the prefix and the other *s* is part of the base word, so both must be there. This will help them remember how to spell the word.

dis-	mis-	pre-	oddball
disagree	**misspell**	**preschool**	precious
dislike	mistreat	prefix	
disable	mismatch	premature	
disobey	misplace	preteen	
discover	misbehave	preview	
dishonest	misjudge	preheat	
disloyal		pretest	
disappear		precaution	
discomfort			

Extend

The game Prefix Spin, described in *WTW*, is recommended to review the prefixes in these first two sorts (*re-*, *un-*, *dis-*, *mis-*, and *pre-*). Students will be able to see how the same base words and prefixes can be used in many different combinations to form words with meanings that they can understand. The base word *cover*, for example, can be used to form *recover*, *uncover*, and *discover*.

Additional Words.   *discharge, discolor, discontent, disorder, displace, distaste, distrust, misdeed, misfit, misguide, mislead, misprint, precook, predate, prepay, preset, prewash, prehistoric*

SORT 48   PREFIXES (*EX-, NON-, IN-, FORE-*)

(See page 113.) Introduce this sort in a manner similar to Sort 46. The prefix *ex-* has subtle variations but generally means "out" or "beyond" in these words. *Non-* means "not," and *fore-* means "before" or "in front of." The prefix *in-* has two distinct meanings: "not" as in *incomplete* and "in" or "into" as in *indent*. Explain to your students that these words are all made up of prefixes but that the rest of the word is not always a base word that stands alone. For example, they will know that *exit* means to "go out" even though *-it* does not have a related meaning. Students will know the meaning of *indenting* a paragraph. They might be interested in learning that *dent* is related to *dentist* and *dental* coming from the Latin word for *tooth*. In a sense when they *indent* they take a bite into the paragraph.

ex-	non-	in-	fore-
exit	**nonsense**	**incomplete**	**forecast**
extend	nonfiction	incorrect	forearm
extra	nonstop	indecent	forehead
express	nonfat	income	foresee
exclude		indoor	foreshadow
exclaim		indent	foremost
expand		insight	

Additional Words.   *explore, exceed, exhale, exile, expel, extra, excavate, exhaust, nonprofit, nonstick, nonviolent, nonskid, inhuman, informal, insane, invisible, inhabit, invade, inmate, inland, inflate, inlaid, ingrown, infield*

SORT 49 PREFIXES (*UNI-*, *BI-*, *TRI-*, AND OTHER NUMBERS)

Demonstrate, Sort, Check, and Reflect

(See page 114.) Introduce this sort in a manner similar to other sorts in this unit. Students will learn that *uni-* means "one," *bi-* means "two," *tri-* means "three," *quad-* means "four," *pent-* means "five," and *oct-* means "eight." Explain that in ancient calendars, October was the eighth month, unlike the modern calendar in which it is the tenth month.

uni-	bi-	tri-	other
unicycle	**bicycle**	**tricycle**	**quadrangle**
united	biweekly	trilogy	pentagon
unicorn	bisect	triangle	octagon
unique	bilingual	triple	octopus
union		triplet	October
unison		tripod	
uniform		trio	
universe			

Extend

Draw attention to the word *bilingual* and find out how many students you have who are or know someone who is bilingual. Remind students of words they studied earlier, like *penguin* and *language,* in which the *gu* had the sound of /gw/. It may be difficult for students to find more words with these prefixes in their reading. Work on developing the meaning and origins of words in the sort by having students look some up in the dictionary and use them in sentences. They will probably know what a *unicorn* is, but a dictionary with etymologies will reveal that *corn* is related to *horn* and that *unicorn* means "one horn."

Additional Words.   *biceps, biped, biplane, bifocals, unify, unity, universal, triceratops, trivet, triad, trinity, trillion*

SORT 50 SUFFIXES (*-Y, -LY, -ILY*)

Demonstrate

(See page 115.) In this sort and the ones that follow, attention shifts to the suffixes. Prepare a set of words to use for teacher-directed modeling. Save the discussion of word meanings until after sorting. Display a transparency of the words on the overhead or hand out the sheet of words to the students. Ask the students what they notice about the words and get ideas about how the words can be sorted. Students might note that all the words end in *y* and contain base words that they recognize. Put up the headers and key words and then sort the rest of the words. Introduce the term **suffix** as a part that is added to the end of a word. Help students think about what the final *-y*, *-ly*, and *-ily* do to the words by talking about the meaning and use of the words. Summarize by explaining that *-y* turns a noun like *sun* into an adjective that means "like the sun" or "having sun," whereas *-ly* and *-ily* turn adjectives like *slow* into adverbs that describe "how" something is done or "the manner in which" something is done. (In the case of *daily* and *nightly*, *-ly* indicates "when.") Students might add these terms to the headers as reminders.

-y		-ly		-ily
sunny	stormy	**slowly**	loudly	**happily**
rainy	chilly	quickly	daily	easily
foggy	cloudy	clearly	roughly	angrily
snowy	windy	dimly	smoothly	lazily
misty	breezy	quietly		noisily

Sort, Check, and Reflect

Have students repeat the sort using the same headers and key words. To reinforce the idea of the base words you might suggest underlining them. This will raise questions about the base word in *happily*, for example, and how it was changed before adding *-ly*. Have students write in the base word for the *-ily* words because they cannot simply underline them. Encourage students to reflect by asking them how the words in each column are alike and what they have learned about adding *-y* and *-ly* to base words.

Extend

To review parts of speech, create frame sentences such as: *Today is _____.* and *He walked _____.* Ask students to find adjectives that describe the noun *today* and adverbs that modify the verb *walk*.

Review with students how to add *-ing* and *-ed* to words like *stop*. Ask them to find two words in the sort that had to double the final letter before adding a suffix (*sunny*, *foggy*). Point out that the word *dim* did not have to double before adding *-ly* because it does not begin with a vowel. Review how to form the plural of words like *party* and *baby* (change the *y* to *i* and add *-es*) and how to make the past tense of words like *carry* and *fly* (change the *y* to *i* and add *-ed*). Ask them to find words in the sort that also had to change the *y* to *i* (this includes *daily*). Help them articulate a new rule about adding *-ly* to words that end in *-y*.

Give students transfer words to practice applying the rules. Ask them to add *-y* or *-ly* to the following base words: *bog (boggy), run (runny), nip (nippy), bug (buggy), dust (dusty), bump (bumpy), soap (soapy), kind (kindly), bad (badly), nice (nicely), noise (noisy), thirst (thirsty), busy (busily), hasty (hastily), hungry (hungrily)*.

Review antonyms by asking students to find opposites among the words in this sort: *slowly/quickly, clearly/dimly, quietly/loudly, smoothly/roughly*. Have students look for weather-related words: *foggy, sunny, rainy, snowy, misty, stormy, chilly, cloudy, windy, breezy*.

SORT 51   COMPARATIVES (-*ER*, -*EST*)

Demonstrate, Sort, Check, and Reflect

(See page 116.) Introduce this sort in a manner similar to Sort 50, reviewing the term **suffix**. Sort first by *-er* and *-est* and talk about the meaning of the words and what the suffix does to the base word. (When comparing two things *-er* is used. When comparing more than two things use *-est*.) Ask students to underline the base words to highlight the fact that the base word in *happier* or *happiest* has been changed. Sort these words into two new categories under *-ier* and *-iest*. Ask students to form a generalization that covers these words and remind them of previous sorts. Add to the generalization you formed with Sort 50 (when a word ends in *-y*, change the *y* to *i* before adding *-ly*, *-ed*, *-es*, *-er*, or *-est*).

-er	-est	-ier	-iest
braver	**bravest**	**happier**	**happiest**
calmer	calmest	easier	easiest
closer	closest	prettier	prettiest
stronger	strongest	crazier	craziest
cooler	coolest	dirtier	dirtiest
hotter	hottest		
weaker	weakest		

Extend

To review the rules involved in adding suffixes, sort the words as follows:

double	e-drop	change *y* to *i*	nothing
hotter	braver	happier	calmer
	closer	easier	stronger
		prettier	cooler
		crazier	weaker
		dirtier	

To help students **transfer** their understanding of these rules to new words ask them to add *-er* and *-est* to these words: *fat, juicy, rough, sunny, flat, lazy, brave, safe, noisy, fine, sad, light, funny,* and *lucky.*

The book *Things That Are Most in the World* by Judi Barrett raises questions about superlatives on each page (What is the smelliest thing in the world) and supplies an answer (a skunk convention). It may inspire your students to create pages for their own version. What is the dirtiest thing in the world? What is the lightest thing in the world?

SORT 52   SUFFIXES (-*NESS*, -*FUL*, AND -*LESS*)

Demonstrate, Sort, Check, and Reflect

(See page 117.) Students should be able to do this as a student-centered sort and establish the categories for themselves. Discuss with students how suffixes change the meaning and use of the word. The suffix *-ness* creates nouns out of adjectives and suggests a "state of being." The suffixes *-ful* and *-less* create adjectives that mean "full of" or "having," and "without." Point out that the suffix is spelled with one *l*.

Draw students' attention to the base words and ask them to find any that have been changed before adding these suffixes. They should see that words ending in a consonant or *e* simply add the endings that start with consonants and do not require any such changes. However, base words that end in *y* must change the *y* to *i* (*happiness, plentiful,* and *penniless*).

-*ness*	-*ful*	-*less*	combination of suffixes
darkness	**graceful**	**homeless**	**carelessness**
goodness	colorful	hopeless	thankfulness
weakness	faithful	worthless	helplessness
illness	thoughtful	restless	peacefulness
kindness	painful	penniless	
happiness	fearful	harmless	
	dreadful		
	plentiful		

Extend

Have students cut apart the base word and suffixes and recombine them to create even more words: *homeless/homelessness, faithful/faithfulness, hopeless/hopelessness*; and to create antonym pairs like *careless/careful, painful/painless, fearful/fearless*.

Additional Words. *awareness, freshness, thankless, thoughtless, painless, fearless, careless, useless, grateful, boastful, truthful, hopeful, restful, helpful, harmful, usefulness, powerless, thoughtfulness, fearlessness, truthfulness, hopelessness, helplessness*

SPELL CHECK 7   ASSESSMENT FOR AFFIXES

Retention Test

The words below have been selected from previous lessons. Call them aloud for students to spell on a sheet of notebook paper and then ask the students to rewrite them into categories and explain why they grouped them together.

1. prefix	**2.** bisect	**3.** uneven	**4.** prettiest
5. octagon	**6.** disloyal	**7.** carelessness	**8.** unicorn
9. expand	**10.** review	**11.** triangle	**12.** misspell
13. quickly	**14.** dirtier	**15.** incorrect	**16.** bravest
17. forehead	**18.** faithful	**19.** nonsense	**20.** noisily

SORT 46   Prefixes (*re-*, *un-*)

re-	*un-*	*oddball*
rebuild	**unable**	recopy
unbeaten	recycle	uncertain
refill	unselfish	reuse
remodel	retrace	uncle
unhappy	unkind	retake
retell	review	unusual
unfair	uneven	rewrite
reptile	unequal	unsteady

SORT 47   Prefixes (*dis-*, *mis-*, *pre-*)

dis-	*mis-*	*pre-*
disagree	**misspell**	**preschool**
mistreat	dislike	prefix
disable	premature	mismatch
preteen	misplace	discover
preview	dishonest	preheat
disloyal	misbehave	precious
discomfort	pretest	disobey
disappear	misjudge	precaution

SORT 48   Prefixes (*ex-*, *non-*, *in-*, *fore-*)

ex-	*non-*	*in-*	*fore-*
exit	nonsense		incomplete
forecast	extend		incorrect
forearm	nonfiction		extra
express	forehead		indecent
foresee	exclude		foreshadow
exclaim	indent		nonstop
insight	income		expand
nonfat	foremost		indoor

SORT 49   Prefixes (*uni-*, *bi-*, *tri-*, and Other Numbers)

uni-	bi-	tri-	other
unicycle	bicycle		tricycle
quadrangle	united		biweekly
trilogy	union		unicorn
bisect	unique		triangle
pentagon	octagon		universe
octopus	unison		triple
uniform	triplet		October
tripod	bilingual		trio

SORT 50   Suffixes (-y, -ly, -ily)

-y	-ly	-ily
sunny	**slowly**	**happily**
quickly	rainy	clearly
snowy	easily	foggy
dimly	misty	quietly
stormy	loudly	angrily
daily	chilly	cloudy
windy	noisily	breezy
roughly	lazily	smoothly

SORT 51   Comparatives (*-er, -est*)

-er	**-est**	**-ier**	**-iest**
braver	**bravest**	**happier**	
happiest	calmer	easier	
calmest	prettier	closer	
closest	easiest	craziest	
stronger	strongest	cooler	
crazier	hotter	prettiest	
coolest	weakest	hottest	
dirtier	weaker	dirtiest	

SORT 52 Suffixes (-ness, -ful, -less)

-ness	-ful	-less	Combination of suffixes
darkness	**graceful**		**homeless**
carelessness	goodness		colorful
thoughtful	faithful		hopeless
thankfulness	painful		weakness
helplessness	illness		restless
harmless	worthless		kindness
peacefulness	penniless		fearful
happiness	plentiful		dreadful

Unit VIII   Miscellaneous Sorts

NOTES FOR THE TEACHER

Background and Objectives

The four sorts in this section are something of a miscellaneous collection that explores different features of words.

Homophones are first introduced in the within word pattern stage and are revisited here with two-syllable words in Sort 53. Chapter 6 in *WTW* describes games and other resources that can be used with this sort. The spelling demons *they're, there,* and *their* are included again even though they were first introduced in the within word pattern stage. **Homographs** are words that are spelled alike but are pronounced differently. Easy homographs often change the sound of the vowel to change the meaning (e.g., I *read* yesterday and I will *read* today. The man with the *bow* tie took a *bow*). The words in Sort 54 vary in meaning according to which syllable is accented (e.g., We plan to *record* a *record*).

Sort 55 looks at words with the *ei* pattern to explore the generalization that the order of letters for the long -*e* sound is "*i* before *e* except after *c*." This sort is included here rather than earlier with other vowel patterns because many of the words that follow the generalization, such as *deceive* and *conceit*, are words more appropriate for older students.

Sorting words by syllables in Sort 56 is placed here to serve as a bridge to the longer words explored in the derivational relations stage and because it includes words more appropriate for upper elementary and middle grades. In this sort, geographical terms are included as words often assigned for spelling in the upper grades. The word *Europe* repeats from earlier. Students will:

- Identify homophones and homographs
- Segment words by syllables
- Spell the words in these sorts

Targeted Learners

These sorts are included here at the end of the syllables and affixes stage because many of the words reflect a more sophisticated vocabulary than words in earlier sorts. However, teachers can use their own judgment about using these sorts earlier in the sequence if they feel it is appropriate. There is no spell check for this unit.

Teaching Tips

The standard weekly routines described on pages 6–7 should be used with these sorts but blind sorts or no-peeking sorts will not work easily for Sorts 53 and 54. Word hunts may not turn up many new words for some of these sorts.

SORT 53   HOMOPHONES

Demonstrate, Sort, Check, and Reflect

(See page 124.) There are 27 words in this week's sort, but some of them repeat from earlier sorts (*choose, flower, higher, very,* and *weather*). No headers are provided because the sorting activity consists of matching word pairs. Present a pair of words like *berry* and *bury*. Ask students what they notice about them (they sound alike but are spelled differently). If students do not know the term **homophone,** supply the word. Continue to pair up words and to talk about what the words mean. Students will typically know one homophone better than the other, but by pairing them up to compare spelling and by discussing their meaning, the new words will become familiar.

Ask students for ideas about how certain spellings can be remembered: *Sellers* have *sales* while *cellers* might have jail *cells; there* has the little word *here* as in "here and there"; one of the *ss* deserted in *desert,* and so on.

berry	bury	vary	very	
cellar	seller	hire	higher	
weather	whether	desert	dessert	
allowed	aloud	metal	medal	
flour	flower	chews	choose	
bored	board	merry	marry	
		they're	there*	their*

*High-frequency word

Extend

Draw small pictures on word cards or in word study notebooks to stimulate memory for the meaning of the word (e.g., draw a strawberry for *berry* and a tombstone for *bury*). Also, have students use these words in sentences. Pairs of students might be assigned three to six words and asked to compose sentences. They might be challenged to make up sentences that contain both of the words such as: *I was not sure whether the weather would be good enough to plan a party outdoors.* The students can share these sentences with each other orally.

Although a word hunt may turn up few additional homophones, students can set up a special section of their word study notebooks in which to record homophones they brainstorm or encounter over time. These should not be limited to two-syllable homophones. Instead of a blind or no-peeking sort partners can turn their words over and play Memory or Concentration to find homophone pairs. Homophone Solitaire is described in Chapter 7 of *WTW.* Homophone Rummy and Win, Lose, or Draw, described in Chapter 6 of *WTW,* will review and extend the study of homophones.

Additional Two-syllable Homophones.   *morning/mourning, ceiling/sealing, cereal/serial, naval/navel, pedal/peddle, profit/prophet, symbol/cymbal, lessen/lesson*

SORT 54   HOMOGRAPHS

Demonstrate, Sort, Check, and Reflect

(See page 125.) In these words the accented syllable is in bold type. Stressed syllables can also be marked with accent marks or underlined. Begin by writing up a sentence such as: *He will present you with a present.* Ask students what they notice about the words *pre sent'* and *pres' ent.* They should note that the words are spelled the same but sound slightly different. Review words such as *wind, lead,* and *read* and introduce the term **homograph,** which means "same writing" or "same spelling." (You might point out how this term is related to *homophone,* which means "same sound.") Go back to the sentence and ask students to identify the part of speech for each word and place the words under the headers *noun* and *verb.* Proceed in a similar manner with each set of words, using them in sentences or inviting students to use them and then to sort them under the headings. When all the words have been sorted, read down each column, placing extra emphasis on the accented syllable. Ask students what they notice. (The nouns are accented on the first syllable and the verbs on the second syllable.)

noun	verb
present	pre**sent**
desert	de**sert**
record	re**cord**
permit	per**mit**
rebel	re**bel**
object	ob**ject**
subject	sub**ject**
reject	re**ject**
produce	pro**duce**
conduct	con**duct**
export	ex**port**
contract	con**tract**

Extend

Partners in a no-peeking or blind sort will have to pronounce the words carefully and perhaps use them in a sentence before asking their buddy to sort them by stress. Ask students to work together to create sentences for these words and to record some of these sentences in their word study notebooks. Students might also draw small pictures as described for homophones above. Homograph Concentration, described in Chapter 7 of *WTW,* is appropriate for review.

SORT 55 *I* BEFORE *E* EXCEPT AFTER *C*

Demonstrate

(See page 126.) This is best done as a teacher-directed sort because it involves several steps. Begin by going over the words to pronounce and talk about the meaning of any words students might not know. Next, model a **sound sort** by putting up the key words *thief* and *neighbor.* Ask students to listen for the vowel sound in each word (long -*e* and long -*a*), and then sort the rest of the words with the students' help by the sound of the vowel in the accented syllable. The word *mischief* will be an oddball. Next, ask students to look for the pattern of letters that spells the vowel sound. Use *thief* and *seize* as key words for long -*e* and sort the rest of the words under them. Explain that not knowing whether to use *ie* or *ei* makes these words difficult to spell correctly, because the sound is the same. However, there is one thing that will help. Ask the students to look for words in which the *ei* comes after the letter *c.* Put these words in another column and put up the headers. The sort will now look something like the following:

ie = long *-e*	*ei* = long *-e*	*cei* = long *-e*	*ei* = long *-a*	oddball
thief	**seize**	**receive**	**neighbor**	mischief
niece	weird	ceiling	eighteen	
priest	either	deceive	weigh	
grief	neither	conceit	sleigh	
shield		receipt	freight	
relieve			reign	
yield				
belief				

Sort, Check, and Reflect

After modeling the sort, have students cut apart and shuffle their own cards and sort them using the same headers and key words. Get students to talk about the categories in their own words and then introduce the old rule: *i* before *e* except after *c* and when sounded as *a* as in *neighbor* and *weigh*. Talk about how well this rule covers the words in the sort. (It does not account for the words under *seize*.) Explain that the rule does help spellers to remember how to spell the words that have *cei*, but we just have to memorize how to spell the others. The silent *p* in *receipt* should be noted.

Extend

Standard weekly routines that include blind sorts or no-peeking sorts will give students practice in mastering these words. Word hunts will not turn up much because there are really only a small number of words spelled with *ei* and *ie*. A few more include *deceit*, *eight, eighty,* and *leisure.*

SORT 56   GEOGRAPHY SYLLABLE SORT

Demonstrate, Sort, Check, and Reflect

(See page 127.) Students will first sort these words by the number of syllables. Expect some disagreement about words like *temperature*. After modeling several words under each header, turn the sorting over to the students. Identify any syllables that might be challenging to spell (such as the first syllable in *island* or the last syllable in *Australia*). Help students see that careful pronunciations of words like *temperature* will help them spell the word. You might speculate about why there is an *e* in *ocean*. (It keeps the *c* soft before the following *a.*) Compare to *ocean* without an *e*—*ocan*. Ask students to pull out the words that name continents and point out the similar spelling in the last syllable of *Africa, America,* and *Antarctica.* (Note that *America* occurs twice so that *North* and *South* can be added to name the two continents in the Western Hemisphere in the concept sort described below.) Read the words to identify the stressed syllable and have students mark the syllable by underlining it on their word cards. Use the dictionary to resolve disputes and introduce the idea of primary and secondary accent in words with more than two syllables.

Two syllables	Three syllables	Four syllables
ocean	**continent**	**geography**
island	hemisphere	environment
Europe	Atlantic	America
climate	Australia	population
Arctic	tropical	information
Asia	Indian	temperature
	equator	Antarctica
	Pacific	peninsula
	Africa	America

Extend

To develop the meanings of these words ask students to work with them in a concept sort. *Continent, ocean,* and *geography* could be used as headers again, but this time related terms will be sorted under each. Add *North* and *South* to the two *America* word cards to sort under *continent. Geography* could include terms like *island* and *peninsula*. Later challenge students to use two, three, four, and even five words at a time in sentences such as: *Africa is a continent on the equator with a tropical climate.*

continent	ocean	geography
Arctic	Pacific	climate
Asia	Indian	tropical
Australia	Atlantic	equator
Africa		population
Antartica		temperature
Europe		peninsula
North America		island
South America		hemisphere
		environment

Students can look for more four-syllable words, or even five-syllable words, in word hunts. Stressbusters or any follow-the-path game board can be adapted to reinforce syllabication. Students move around the board according to the number of syllables they can count in the word cards they draw.

SORT 53 Homophones

berry	bury	cellar
very	seller	flour
weather	bored	vary
hire	desert	board
flower	whether	metal
chews	higher	aloud
allowed	dessert	medal
merry	choose	marry
they're	there	their

SORT 54   Homographs

noun	verb	
present	pre**sent**	**des**ert
re**cord**	per**mit**	re**bel**
permit	de**sert**	**rec**ord
rebel	sub**ject**	**ob**ject
reject	ob**ject**	**sub**ject
produce	con**duct**	**ex**port
conduct	re**ject**	pro**duce**
contract	ex**port**	**con**tract

SORT 55 *i before e* Except After *c*

ie = /e/	*cei* = /e/	*ei* = /e/	*ei* = /a/
thief	**receive**	**neighbor**	
seize	niece	ceiling	
eighteen	weigh	priest	
deceive	weird	sleigh	
grief	shield	either	
receipt	mischief	relieve	
yield	belief	freight	
neither	reign	conceit	

SORT 56   Geography Syllable Sort

2 syllables	3 syllables	4 syllables
ocean	**continent**	**geography**
climate	Antarctica	environment
Asia	Indian	population
peninsula	America	hemisphere
Atlantic	Pacific	information
Arctic	tropical	Australia
Europe	Africa	temperature
equator	island	America

Appendix

Blank Template for Word Sorts

Independent Word Study Form

Word Sort Corpus

Blank Template for Word Sorts

Independent Word Study Form

Name _____ Date _____

Cut apart your words and sort them first. Then write your words below under a key word.

_____

_____

_____

_____

_____

_____

_____

_____

_____

_____

_____

What did you learn about words from this sort?

_____

_____

_____

On the back of this paper write the same key words you used above. Ask someone to shuffle your word cards and call them aloud as you write them into categories. Look at each word as soon as you write it. Correct it if needed.

Check off what you did and ask a parent to sign below.
_____ Sort the words again in the same categories you did in school.
_____ Write the words in categories as you copy the words.
_____ Do a no-peeking sort with someone at home.
_____ Write the words into categories as someone calls them aloud.
_____ Find more words in your reading that have the same sound and/or pattern. Add them to the categories on the back.

Signature of Parent _____

Word Sort Corpus: Numbers refer to the sort in which the word appears

able	29	Asia	56	bisect	49	castle	44
*about	22	ask	2	biweekly	49	catalog	41
acted	5	asking	2	blanket	13	catcher	33
actor	32	assign	44	bled	6	cattle	30
actress	40	athlete	15	bleed	6	caught	45
adding	4	Atlantic	56	board	53	caution	23
address	40	attack	42	body	36	ceiling	55
adhere	28	attic	42	bookcase	10	cellar	53
adore	25	auction	23	bookmark	10	cement	39
advice	18	August	23	bookworm	10	central	39
afraid	38	Australia	56	bored	25, 53	century	39
Africa	56	author	23	bottle	29	cereal	39
*after	13	autumn	23	bottom	13	certain	27
*again	17	avoid	22	bought	44	changes	7
against	38	awake	17	bouquet	43	chapter	13
agreed	38	aware	24	bowling	19	checkout	11
airplane	24	*away	38	bracelet	17	cheerful	28
all right	23	awesome	23	branches	7	cherry	36
allow	22	awful	23	brave	1	chewed	5
allowed	53	awhile	38	braver	51	chews	53
almost	23	awkward	23	bravest	51	chewy	20
alone	19	awoke	19	breezy	50	chicken	42
*along	38	backward	26	bridle	29	chief	1
aloud	38, 53	bacon	34	brief	1	children	15
alphabet	45	ballet	35	brighter	32	chilly	50
already	23	balloon	20	brightly	18	chocolate	17
*also	23	bandage	40	broken	34	choose	53
although	23	bandit	35	brought	44	chorus	25
*always	23	banquet	43	brownie	36	chosen	34
amaze	17	barber	24	brushes	7	churches	7
America	56	barely	24	buckle	42	cider	39
among	38	bargain	34	budget	40	circle	39
amount	22	basement	17	buffet	35	classes	7
amuse	20	battle	29	bugle	29	clean	3
angel	30	beauty	20	burglar	32	cleaned	16
angle	30	*because	38	bury	53	cleaning	16
angrily	50	*before	25	butter	13	clearly	50
annoy	22	beggar	32	cabin	34	climate	35, 56
*another	38	begging	4	cable	29	*clothes	7
answer	44	belief	55	calmer	51	climb	1
Antarctica	56	believe	38	calmest	51	clog	1
antique	43	below	19	cancel	30	close	3
anyone	11	benches	7	candle	29	closed	5
*anything	11	beneath	38	candy	36	closer	51
appear	28	berry	36, 53	captain	34	closest	51
apple	29	beside	11, 18	capture	33	closet	35
appoint	22	*better	13	career	28	closing	3
approach	19	between	38	careful	24	cloudy	50
April	30	beware	24	carelessness	52	coaster	19
Arctic	56	beyond	38	carpet	24	cocoon	20
argue	41	bicycle	49	carried	37	collar	31
*around	22	bigger	32	carries	37	collect	39
arrive	18	bilingual	49	*carry	24	college	39
ashes	7	birdbath	27	carrying	37	*color	31
ashore	25	birthday	27	cartoon	20	colorful	52

*Words that occur in the top 300 high-frequency words

combine	18	cyclist	39	downpour	10	explode	19
comet	35	daily	50	downstairs	10	explore	25
coming	4	dairy	24	downtown	10	export	54
common	39	dancer	32	dragon	34	express	48
compare	24	danger	33	draw	6	extend	48
compass	40	darkness	52	dreadful	52	extra	48
compete	21	daughter	45	dream	3	extreme	21
complain	17	daylight	10	dreamer	32	fabric	42
complete	15	debate	38	dreaming	3	faded	16
complex	42	decay	17	dreary	28	failure	33
compose	19	decayed	37	drew	6	fairy	24
conceit	55	decaying	37	drive	6	faithful	52
conduct	54	decays	37	driver	32	farmer	32
confuse	20	deceive	55	driveway	18	fasten	44
conquer	43	decide	18	dropped	5	father	31
contain	17	declare	24	drove	6	fatigue	41
contest	39	decode	19	drowsy	22	faucet	23
continent	56	deer	8	duet	15	favor	31
contract	54	defeat	21	during	27	favorite	18
control	15	defend	38	dwarf	26	fearful	52
cookbook	10	degree	38	*early	28	feather	21
cookie	36	delight	18	earthquake	28	feature	21
cooler	51	deny	36	easier	51	feeling	4
coolest	51	depend	38	easiest	51	feet	8
copied	37	describe	18	easily	50	female	13
copies	37	desert	53, 54	eastern	21	fever	13
copying	37	design	44	easy	14	fewer	20
corncob	25	desire	38	eat	3	fifteen	21
corner	25	despair	24	eating	3	figure	33
correct	39	dessert	53	edit	35	final	30
cotton	34	destroy	22	eerie	36	finish	14
cougar	20	develop	38	eighteen	55	firmly	27
cough	45	dialog	41	either	55	fixing	4
countdown	10	diet	15	elephant	45	flashlight	10
counter	22	dimly	50	eleven	34	flawless	23
county	22	diner	12	employ	22	floated	16
couple	30	dinner	12	English	15	floating	4
courage	40	dirtier	51	enjoyed	37	florist	25
cousin	34	dirtiest	51	enjoying	37	flour	53
cover	31	dirty	27	enjoys	37	flower	31, 53
coward	22	disagree	47	enough	45	finger	13
cradle	29	disappear	47	environment	56	foggy	50
crashes	7	discomfort	47	equal	43	follow	13
crayon	17	discover	47	equator	56	foot	8
crazier	51	dishonest	47	erode	19	forearm	48
craziest	51	dislike	47	escape	17	forecast	48
crazy	12	disloyal	47	Europe	19, 56	forehead	48
create	15	disobey	47	even	12	foremost	48
creature	33	distance	40	everyone	11	foresee	48
credit	35	ditches	7	everything	11	foreshadow	48
cried	9	dizzy	36	evil	30	forest	25
cruel	15	doctor	31	example	56	forgive	18
cry	9	dollar	31	exclaim	48	forty	25
crying	9	dolphin	45	exclude	48	fossil	30
culture	33	donkey	36	excuse	20	fought	45
curtain	34	doodle	20	exit	48	fountain	34
custom	39	double	22	expand	48	foxes	7
cutting	4	downhill	10	explain	17	fragile	30

meeting	14	neither	55	passing	2	postage	19
member	13	nephew	45	pasture	33	poster	19
mercy	28	nervous	27	pattern	13	posture	33
merely	28	*never	14	pavement	17	powder	22
merit	35	nickel	42	payment	17	practice	40
mermaid	27	niece	55	peacefulness	52	precaution	47
merry	53	ninety	18	peanut	14	precious	47
message	40	nodded	5, 16	pearly	28	prefix	47
metal	30, 53	noisily	50	pencil	30	preheat	47
metric	42	nonfat	48	penguin	34	premature	47
mice	8	nonfiction	48	penniless	52	preschool	47
middle	29	nonsense	48	peninsula	56	*present	14, 54
midget	40	nonstop	48	pentagon	49	pressure	33
minute	14	noodle	20	*people	21	preteen	47
mirror	31	normal	25	perfect	27	pretest	47
misbehave	47	northern	25	perform	25	prettier	51
mischief	55	noisy	22	perhaps	27	prettiest	51
misjudge	47	nothing	11	permit	54	*pretty	12
mismatch	47	notice	40	perplex	42	preview	47
misplace	47	novel	30	person	27	priest	55
mission	34	number	13	phantom	45	princess	40
misspell	47	obey	17	phone	1, 45	prison	34
mistake	17	obeyed	37	photocopy	45	private	35
mistreat	47	obeying	37	phrase	45	problem	13
misty	50	oatmeal	19	physics	45	produce	54
mitten	34	obeys	37	pick	2	provide	18
mixed	5	object	54	picking	2	pumpkin	15
mixes	7	ocean	56	pickle	42	puppy	12
mixture	33	octagon	49	picnic	42	purple	27
moan	3	octopus	49	picture	33	purpose	27
moaning	3	October	49	pilgrim	15	pushing	4
model	30	office	40	pillow	13	quadrangle	49
moisture	22	often	44	pilot	14	quaint	43
moment	13	older	32	pinkie	36	quality	43
*money	36	*only	13	pirate	35	quarrel	26
monkey	36	*open	12	pitcher	33	quarter	26
monster	15	orbit	35	places	7	queasy	43
*morning	25	*order	25	plague	41	question	43
mosquito	43	orphan	45	planet	14	quick	42
*mother	31	*other	31	planned	5	quickly	50
motor	31	outside	11	plastic	42	quiet	35
mountain	34	*over	12	play	7	quietly	50
mouse	8	owner	19	played	9	quit	1
movie	36	Pacific	56	playing	9	quiver	43
moving	4	package	40	plays	9	quizzes	43
muffin	34	paddle	29	pleasant	21	quote	1
muscle	29	painful	52	pleasure	33	quoted	16
mushroom	15	painted	16	plentiful	52	rabbit	12
music	14	painter	17	plot	1	raccoon	20
*myself	11	panting	16	plotting	16	racket	35
named	5	paper	12	pocket	42	racing	16
napkin	34	parade	17	poem	15	racquet	43
nature	33	paragraph	45	poet	15	rainbow	17
naughty	45	pardon	24	poison	22	rainy	50
nearby	28	parents	24	police	40	raisin	17
needed	16	partner	24	polite	18	rancher	33
needle	21	pass	2	pollute	20	rather	31
neighbor	55	passed	5	population	56	reader	21

reading	4	sample	29	sketches	7	stayed	9
reason	14	saucer	23	skipped	16	staying	9
rebel	54	sausage	23	sleep	6	stays	9
rebuild	46	saved	5	sleigh	55	steady	21
receipt	55	saving	16	slept	6	stepped	5
receive	55	say	6	slid	6	stirred	5
recess	40	scale	1	slide	6	stolen	34
recopy	46	science	40	slightly	18	stomach	42
record	25, 54	scooter	20	slowly	50	stopping	4
recycle	46	scored	5	smaller	32	stormy	50
reduce	20	scout	1	smell	1	story	36
refill	46	scrapbook	10	smoother	32	strays	9
refuse	20	scratches	7	smoothly	50	strong	41
rehearse	28	season	21	sneaker	14	stronger	51
reign	55	*second	14	snowflake	10	strongest	51
reject	54	secret	35	snowing	4	student	14
relax	42	seemed	5	snowman	10	studied	37
relieve	55	seize	55	snowplow	10	studies	37
remain	17	seller	53	snowstorm	10	study	27
remodel	46	senate	35	soapy	19	studying	37
remote	19	senior	33	soften	44	stupid	13
repair	24	sentence	40	solar	31	subject	54
repeat	21	sequel	43	soldier	19	succeed	21
replied	37	sequence	43	somebody	11	sugar	31
replies	37	sermon	28	somehow	11	summer	12
reply	36	serpent	28	someone	11	summit	35
replying	37	service	27	something	11	sunlight	10
report	25	setting	4	sometime	11	sunny	50
reptile	46	settle	29	somewhere	11	super	12
request	43	*seven	14	sooner	32	supper	12
require	43	severe	28	sorry	25	suppose	19
resign	44	shampoo	20	southern	22	surgeon	40
rest	2	sharp	1	spearmint	28	surprise	18
resting	2	sheep	8	special	30	survive	18
restless	52	shield	55	speeches	7	swarm	26
retake	46	shine	6	spelling	4	sweater	21
retell	46	shock	42	spider	31	sweep	6
retrace	46	shone	6	spied	9	swimmer	32
reuse	46	shopper	32	spies	9	swimming	2
review	46	shorter	25	spirit	27	table	29
reward	25	shouted	5	splashes	7	taking	4
rewrite	46	shouting	16	spray	9	talking	4
rhyme	44	shrug	41	sprayed	9	target	35
rhythm	44	shut	2	spraying	9	taught	45
ribbon	34	shutting	2	spy	9	teacher	33
rifle	29	sidewalk	18	spyed	9	teardrop	28
riot	15	sideways	11	squabble	26	technique	43
river	14	signal	30	squad	26	teeth	8
rocket	35	silent	13	squash	26	telling	16
rooster	20	silver	31	squat	26	temperature	56
rough	45	simple	29	squeaky	43	thank	1
roughly	50	sincere	28	squirm	43	thankfulness	52
ruler	12	single	29	squirrel	43	*their	53
rumor	31	*sister	13	stain	1	theme	1
running	2	sitting	2	stand	2	themselves	11
saddle	30	skate	3	standing	2	*there	53
said	6	skated	16	started	5	thermos	28
sailor	32	skating	3	stay	9	they're	53

Word		Word		Word		Word	
*thief	55	trio	49	useful	20	window	13
thirsty	27	triple	49	using	3	windy	50
thirteen	21	triplet	49	vague	41	winning	16
thirty	27	tripod	49	valley	36	winter	13
*though	44	triumph	45	vary	53	without	11
thoughtful	52	trophy	45	*very	36, 53	wives	8
thousand	22	trouble	22	village	40	wolf	8
threw	6	trust	1	visit	14	wolves	8
through	44	Tuesday	20	voices	7	*woman	8
throughout	11	turkey	36	volley	36	women	8
throw	6	turtle	27	voter	32	worker	26
Thursday	27	tutor	32	vowel	30	working	4
ticket	42	twenty	36	voyage	22	world	26
tiger	12	twig	1	waffle	26	worse	26
tiny	12	unable	46	wagon	14	worship	26
title	29	unbeaten	46	waited	5	worthless	52
toaster	19	uncertain	46	wander	26	worthwhile	26
*today	17	uncle	46	wanted	5	worthy	26
tongue	41	*under	31	warden	26	worry	26
tooth	8	unequal	46	wardrobe	26	wrap	1
toothache	20	uneven	46	warmth	26	wrapped	16
topic	42	unfair	46	warning	26	wreckage	44
torture	33	unhappy	46	warrior	26	wrestle	44
total	30	unicorn	49	watch	26	wrinkle	44
tough	45	unicycle	49	watches	7	write	3
toward	24	uniform	49	*water	13	writer	32
tractor	31	union	49	wave	3	writing	3
trade	3	unique	49	waving	3	yearbook	28
trading	3	unison	49	weaker	51	yearn	28
traffic	42	united	49	weakest	51	yell	2
traitor	32	universe	49	weakness	52	yelling	2
tranquil	43	unkind	46	weather	31, 53	*yellow	13
travel	30	unit	35	weigh	55	yield	55
treasure	33	unselfish	46	weird	55	younger	32
tremble	29	unsteady	46	when	1	yourself	11
trial	15	*until	30	whether	53	zigzag	41
triangle	49	unusual	46	whine	1		
tricycle	49	*upon	38	whistle	44		
trilogy	49	use	2	wife	8		